*connecting! We
need to hear all
you have to say!*

CONNECT!
A Simple Guide to Public Speaking for Writers

*Blessings,
Linda Apple
6/14/13*

CONNECT!
A Simple Guide to Public Speaking for Writers

Linda C. Apple

AWOC.COM Publishing
Denton, Texas

AWOC.COM Publishing
P.O. Box 2819
Denton, TX 76202

Manufactured in the United States of America

ISBN: 978-0-937660-62-1

Visit Linda C. Apple's web site: www.LindaCApple.com

Dedication

This book is dedicated to my precious friend, Cozy Dixon, who first gave me an opportunity to speak, and a safe place to fail. Her wisdom, support and unyielding faith helped to inspire who I am today.

A Special Note of Thanks

Thank you, Neal, for being my biggest supporter, and dearest friend. If it weren't for you, I would have never thought of this book in the first place.

Thank you, my sweet "earth" friends, Ann Holbrook and Linda Manire, for wading through my "windy" creativity and editing this manuscript. You will never know how much I appreciate the hours you spent reading and re-reading each word.

Thank you, Dan. Once again you took a chance on me. I won't let you down. Thank you for all of your hard work on this book.

Table of Contents

Introduction

"If you think you're too small to be effective, you have never been in bed with a mosquito"~ Betty Reese

Why I Wrote this Book

I've been speaking to groups for over twenty-five years, long before I started writing. My speaking career suffered a rocky beginning. The first time I heard my recorded voice on the radio, I hated the way it sounded. Some time later, however, I got over myself. I enjoyed connecting with those in my audience, their enthusiasm inspired me and I knew this was something I wanted to pursue.

I learned about public speaking at my church by teaching a ladies' Bible study. Our pastor's wife, who is also my dear friend, gave me many opportunities to stand before an audience. And what an audience! Those loving and encouraging ladies gave me *a lot* of grace. In that environment I had a safe place to fail. Every time I fell flat on my face, and those times were many, they lifted my spirits and encouraged me to continue.

A few years later, I decided to get professional training and joined Toastmasters. There I learned the techniques for presenting and the elements of an effective speech. Since then I've also attended CLASSeminar given by CLASServices, Inc., a Christian based company.

From my training, I learned how public speaking served many valuable purposes. However, I never really connected my speaking and writing. They were like train tracks that ran parallel and appeared to meet on the horizon. I never thought about the two uniting in my future. Then it happened. The word "platform" kept popping up at conferences and workshops. Terry Burns, my agent, informed his clients about the growing importance of having a platform. He told how editors now expected authors to be highly visible and to take part in selling their own books.

It became clear that, as the cliché goes, writing and speaking were now married. A "hand-in-glove" relationship. This information didn't bother me. I loved microphones!

However, I can't say the same for most of the writers I meet. Microphones terrify most of them. When I speak to a group of writers and I suggest they also try public speaking they look at me like a tree full of owls.

I finally realized most do not have a safe place to fail like I did when I first started speaking. They don't have the support system I had or the encouragement to try again.

That is the reason I'm writing this book. As a writer, you are already skilled at telling stories. You know about the toil, creativity, and research it takes to write a story. Some of you, after a lot of hard work and determination have been successful in being published. Others of you, who have worked just as hard and have just as much determination, feel invisible to editors and agents.

Let's fix that. I've written *Connect!* in a simple, conversational style. It is based on my experiences. I confess my blunders and embarrassing episodes. After a while you will realize that if I can do it, so can you.

In fact, you will probably do it better! At least, that is my goal.

Although this book is focused on the needs of writers, the information is beneficial to anyone who is thinking about becoming a public speaker.

Connect! is a jumping off place. Should you decide you would like to do this professionally, I highly recommend you join Toastmasters and attend various professional speaker seminars.

What you will find in Connect!

Simply Speaking: I cover the reasons why you should speak. Building a platform is just one of those reasons. Speaking leads to personal enrichment and is an opportunity to give back to writers just starting out. It is sort of a "circle of life" for writers.

Finding a Topic: You may feel unqualified to speak because you haven't been published. You may be saying to yourself, "Besides, even if I were published I'd have nothing to talk about." This chapter *sheds* light on why you *are* qualified to speak and how to find several topics from a single article or short story.

Preparing a Speech: This chapter will be familiar to writers. It is about organizing the topic information, fleshing it out, and editing until it is tight. This becomes the script you will use for practice.

Presenting the Speech: I write about overcoming fear as well as what to do before, during, and after your presentation. Think of me being in your corner saying, "You can do this! So you messed up? No biggie. Get up, dust yourself off, learn from it and keep going!"

Finding an Audience: You may get tired of speaking to the person in the mirror. This chapter has several suggestions and ideas on how to get your name in front of event coordinators. I also suggest business tools that will help you accomplish this.

Your Speaking Style: My favorite chapter! It is a fun and eye-opening insight to your communication style. This will also help you understand the members in your audience. You will be able to recognize by their facial expressions and body language if they are with you or drifting away and you will know how to adjust your presentation style to keep everyone's attention. This information also helps you from being offended by the actions and comments of others because you realize they are just "wired" that way.

And Furthermore: Repetition is the best teacher. This chapter lists reminders of things you've already read in previous chapters plus additional recommendations to make your presentations successful.

Connect! Is my pep talk to you, as well as a challenge. I hope this book will be instrumental in some part to your great success and that one day I will be a member of the audience where you are speaking.

Let's get started!

Linda C. Apple~2010

Simply Speaking

"Communication is depositing a part of yourself in another person." Author Unknown

Why speak? I can think of four reasons: building a platform, enhancing our marketing, providing us opportunity for personal enrichment, and allowing us to give back. Speakers benefit from all of the above. I'll explain how.

Building Our Platform

What is a platform? Simply put, it is your visibility and it showcases your ability to market your work. Gone are the days when the writer created the stories and the publisher sold them. Now we also have to create the buzz and sell our work on our own.

Why is a platform important? Let me paint a word picture for you. Imagine a football field jam-packed with writers standing shoulder-to-shoulder, all of them facing west. There is no room to move or turn around. At the west end of the field is a six-foot high stage. On the stage are agents, editors, and readers.

The first two rows in front of the stage are writers Nora Roberts, Stephen King, John Grisham, Tom Clancy, Dan Brown, and other bestselling authors. The next eight rows are filled with people who have published several books and have a following. You, however, are somewhere in the back.

The editors, agents, and readers can see the first few rows without any problem and they recognize those people. However, the writers behind them are faceless. They are the "writing masses."

The first two rows of writers only have to write. Because they are easy to recognize, people buy their books. The eight rows behind them occasionally need to promote their work. But you? You are in that sea of faceless multitude.

Now suppose someone squeezed a ladder in the crowd and leaned it against the tall person in front of you, with their permission of course, and you climbed to the top. Then, while standing above the crowd you waved your arms in big sweeping motions and yelled like your hair was on fire. I guarantee you'd get the attention of the folks on stage!

That is what platform does for you.

Terry Burns, author and agent for Hartline Literary Agency, told me that publishers almost always ask about the author's platform. He has actually pitched a manuscript to editors and although they really liked the story, turned it down because his client didn't have a platform. How sad! Terry also pointed out how it used to be only nonfiction writers who needed a platform. Now it is just as important for fiction writers.

Dan Case, owner and editor of AWOC.COM Publishing, concurs with Terry. As a small press owner, he doesn't have the large sums it takes to promote each author. When an author pitches a book to him at a conference and he is interested, he first asks the prospective author about his or her marketing plan before he accepts the proposal or manuscript. If the person doesn't have a platform, he may turn it down even though he likes the idea.

There are many ways to build a platform. Creating a website, writing a blog, compiling a large email and mailing list, writing newsletters, getting published in newspapers and magazines, using online social networks, and many more things along those lines.

However, public speaking and conducting workshops are by far the best way to gain attention and credibility.

Enhancing Our Marketing

Another good reason to become a speaker is that it enhances our marketing. Not only is it important to a publisher for you to sell your work, it is also important to you, especially if you've self-published.

Let's say you are attending a conference. You pay to rent a table, set it up in the lobby, sit and wait. People pass by and talk with you, pick up your book and thumb through a few pages, then set it down with the promise to return. Some do, most don't. Sound familiar?

However, when you are a presenter and refer to your book, your table will be flocked afterwards. I've found that speaking connects you with audience members and sparks interest better than anything I've ever done.

I attended the Ozarks Creative Writers' Conference in Eureka Springs last fall. I had a table and a few people moseyed by and bought my book, *Inspire! Writing from the Soul.* The last day of the conference, Dusty Richards, the Western Writing god, (he's published 100 books!) conducted a "brag" session at the end of the day. When it came my turn, I stood and told about my book. It took two minutes, max. Afterwards, I sold more books in twenty minutes than I had all weekend!

Opportunity for Personal Enrichment

Another benefit is the personal enrichment you get from speaking. Free travel for instance. Most speakers start locally, but after a while they receive statewide invitations as well as from other states. At the very least, travel expenses are paid by the group holding the event. This is also a great opportunity for writers to get ideas for new stories. You can see places firsthand, make notes, and use them later.

You meet interesting people who are another source of creative information. Speaking to writer's groups is one of my favorite benefits. Have you noticed how there is an electric energy when writers get together? We *get* one other. We sharpen one another and when we return to our computers we are motivated to get back in the chair and pound the keyboard.

Since speaking builds credibility, you will also make important contacts who can help you expand your platform. You might meet someone interested in carrying your book in their store, or buying your work for their club. It may be an established writer who offers to recommend you to their publisher or agent. After you speak, you may have a publisher ask you to write a book about your speech topic. That happened to me. Dan Case knew I spoke about inspirational creative nonfiction writing and he asked me to write a book for him. That is how *Inspire!* came about.

Giving Back

Finally, speaking provides an opportunity for you to "give back." One of my favorite things to do is conducting my inspirational creative nonfiction workshop. It is especially helpful for those who want to be published in anthologies like *Chicken Soup for the Soul* and *Cup of Comfort*. Others simply want to write their life story for their children and grandchildren. This workshop is also good for devotional writing.

The interaction I have with the writers during the workshop is refreshing. There is nothing more gratifying than when a former workshop attendee comes to me and excitedly announces, "Chicken Soup bought my story! I'm getting published and it is all because of your workshop!"

My speaking to writers groups started after I had sold several stories to the Chicken Soup books. A friend asked me, "What's your secret?" I told her how I used the creative nonfiction style of writing.

Of course, she was eager to know all about it and since I'm not one of those writers who fear someone displacing me in the race to be published, we had a cup of coffee and I explained this style of writing. That's when I got the idea of doing this workshop. I wanted to give back and help those who wished to learn about writing, and who desireded to share their life's stories.

I'm so grateful for the writers who have given to me, and still do. Like Velda Brotherton, a dear friend and multi-published novelist. When I decided to try my hand at fiction she met with me one day a week to teach me how to write in this genre and also critiqued what I'd written.

Another one of my writer heroes, Dusty Richards, remembers the difficult path to publishing and how hard it was to take that first step into the world of committed writing. That vulnerable place where, if he wanted to be published, he had to pitch his manuscripts, speak with agents, and take risks. This obviously worked for him. Now he shares his knowledge and drive to help other writers. He pushed Velda through the doorway to being published, and he did the same for me.

I wouldn't be writing today if Lois Spoon, a precious friend who passed years ago, hadn't started a writing group. She also taught me to take a risk, "After all," she'd say, "the worst they could say is 'no.'"

Author and publisher Dan Case gave me the opportunity to write my first book. My agent, Terry

Burns, who is also an author, took a chance and agreed to represent me. All of these writers, and many more, have invested their time and talent in my life. They have helped me find my writing niche and voice.

For those of you who are intimidated by the success of other writers and feel unworthy to offer anything worthwhile, remember this, *no matter who you are there will always be someone better than you, and there will always be someone not as good as you.* We are unique, and we need each other to keep the writer's circle of life going.

Over the years I have met and befriended authors whose books are regular titles on the New York Times bestseller lists and writers who have yet to be published. It doesn't matter on which rung of the publishing ladder we stand, we can all learn from each other. And one way to help writers is to become a speaker.

If you are thinking, "Even if I decided to be a speaker, what on earth would I talk about?" I have some ideas. Follow me to the next chapter.

Finding a Topic

"There are three things to aim at in public speaking: first, to get into your subject, then to get your subject into yourself, and lastly, to get your subject into the heart of your audience." ~ Alexander Gregg

What Will I Talk About?

After selling several stories to the *Chicken Soup for the Soul* books, a small writers' group invited me to speak about writing for that market. Their invitation honored me, but I also felt inadequate. The feeling of incompetency went with me to the meeting like an old buzzard hunched over on my shoulder.

Things changed when I stood to speak. I saw the expectant faces in the group and at that moment I realized I was nothing more than one writer telling other writers how to succeed—simply sharing my experiences, nothing more. I wasn't trying to be the big dollar helping all the little dimes. The presentation was a success. They enjoyed the interaction and we all laughed a lot.

I've learned that our mindset makes all the difference. That is what public speaking should be all about—helping others to succeed. And in doing so, the public speaker succeeds. When talking to someone about speaking I can always count on this question, "What would I talk about?"

My answer? If you think outside the writer's box (or block, whichever the case may be) you will find a wealth of topics. Don't worry, I'll help you.

"But," they counter, "everything has already been talked about by more experienced writers than me. No one wants to hear what I have to say."

To answer that question, I have another word picture. (Can you tell I like those? I'm a very visual person).

Think of a topic as a single beam of light shining through a multifaceted prism. When a beam of light shines through a prism, spectral colors burst out. Red, orange, yellow, green, blue, and violet dance on the walls.

Now let's say each color represents a certain group of people. Each group is of a particular culture, socioeconomic structure, and unique learning and comprehension style.

At a conference or meeting you will have all colors and types of people. The speaker at the conference happens to be a violet speaker. While everyone understands what this speaker is saying, which group really gets it? The violet group. That is because the speaker knows how to communicate with them in their unique language.

There are people who will hear the same information from you that they've heard before, but, because you speak in their unique style, they will "get it." I assure you, there are people out there who need your unique perspective and voice.

There is a proverb that claims there is nothing new under the sun? That is true, however, your perspective will make it seem new. Now, back to finding topics.

Most of the time when someone asks you to speak they already have a topic in mind. However, it is good to have two presentations ready to offer in case one is not suggested or when you are the one offering your services as a speaker.

Topics are easy to find. The reason they seem so hard to come up with is because we put mental barriers around our subject matter. We think that's the only thing we can talk about. But our subject matter is what provides us with a plethora of ideas.

Another reason some feel unqualified to speak is because they aren't published or because they don't have a college degree. That just isn't the case. Writers need to have a platform before they sell. As I said earlier, that is one of the first questions a prospective editor or agent asks. As for not having a degree, the research and time spent on your work definitely qualifies you.

I will use the historical novel I wrote, which was set during the Gold Rush, to illustrate how topics can be found. The story line is about a young woman traveling with her maid to the gold fields to find her father. If I were thinking inside my mental barrier, I would assume the only thing I could talk about is the Gold Rush. But I'm not thinking that. Let's step over the barriers and see what we can find.

It took me a year to research this book. I'm sure I didn't need to take a full year, but I love history and sort of got lost in the process. However, that research provided numerous topics for me to present to a variety of groups.

One topic that stood out was the courage of the women who traveled to the gold fields. These ladies were trained from their youth about social graces, the arts, and keeping a proper home. Many of the women on the trail were from privileged lives with servants. They attended tea parties, musical societies, and dances with their friends. They enjoyed fresh fruit and vegetables in the warm months and the produce they canned for the winter providing them with treats such as pickled peaches, applesauce, and pickles. Life for most was generally good. That is until their husbands got the notion to go West and told the family to pack up. These women had no choice but to go. Everything changed—for the worse. They lived in tents, cooked over open fires, and ate a lot of preserved meat and corndodgers. They bathed in muddy streams and took care of "business" in the bushes, if they were lucky enough to have any around. When there wasn't a private place, the ladies in the wagon train would form a circle facing out and spread their skirts. Then each one took a turn being in the middle to relieve herself. They called it a privacy circle.

They gave birth in wagons, lost children to disease, or literally lost them. There are stories about children wandering away in the tall grasses on the prairie. After a few days of parents unsuccessfully trying to find their child they would have to give up because the wagon train couldn't lose any more time. Can you imagine being a mother knowing that your child is out there somewhere and you are forced to leave?

When they arrived at the gold fields they lived in dark cabins with holes cut out for windows letting in all kinds of bugs. I found it interesting that of all the things these women missed the most, glass in their windows topped their list. One lady hit on the idea of stacking jars in the windows and stuffing moss in the gaps. Instead of having wood floors, they lived on dirt floors. But these ladies were determined to be civilized and swept those dirt floors daily with brush brooms. The cabins were usually one-room structures with blankets dividing off a bedroom. No privacy!

If you think that's bad, imagine this scenario.

Some of these marriages resulted from need. The mortality rate for women was extremely high due to childbirth. If a man's wife died, he needed someone to take care of his children—and families usually consisted of five or more. Widows needed someone to help provide for her large brood. So the two would marry out of necessity—nothing more. Picture a one-room house full of children and your bedroom wall is a blanket. Yikes!

The ladies' pale, soft skin turned brown, hard, and wrinkled. Their clothes were worn and their children were their only companions. That is the main thing that touched my heart—their isolation. I read diaries and letters where they poured out their souls expressing indescribable loneliness. How they longed for female companionship.

So, what topics could I take from this? I could give a presentation about some of the women I read about. I could speak of bravery in hard circumstances and the result of that bravery. How about finding creative solutions to problems? The importance of relationships for women would be a possibility. I could also talk about cooking on the trail, medicines from herbs, fears and folklore, and the impact this movement had on the many Indian tribes.

Places I could give presentations are schools, women's groups—both civic and religious—historical groups, cooking clubs, holistic events, homemaker groups, 4H clubs, and the Scouts. I could speak about how things were done in the 1800's, such as the practice of medicine, cooking, building homes, sewing, and gardening. I could discuss the personalities of the people, their courage, and the challenges they faced and how we could learn from them.

Writer's groups would be interested in how I researched my book, who I interviewed and whether I traveled to the places I wrote about, as well as what I experienced on the trip. They'd like to know about life in the 1800's, and interesting people to use in their character development. I could tell why I chose this subject and about my personal process of writing—how many hours a day I wrote, how I juggled writing and caring for my family, how many rewrites I made, whether I got an agent, and how I marketed my book.

See? There are many things from which to build a presentation. Oh, and I could also talk about the Gold Rush.

Let's say you are a mystery writer. Right away you may think the only group you could speak to are other mystery writers or readers. You'd probably assume your only topic choice would be about your past works or your work in progress. But there is so much more you could talk about! Tell about your research—did you interview people like forensics experts or medical professionals? Speak about those experiences. Tell how you set up the appointment, details of the meeting and the information you gathered. Then explain how you used it in your book or article.

Anecdotes (a story about an interesting or humorous incident from your or someone else's experience) always endear you to the audience.

Just because you are a mystery writer doesn't mean you are limited to writing groups. My friend wrote a cozy mystery about a self-appointed female detective who tried to help a battered woman. While writing her book, she researched the problem of battered women and shelters. She also looked into the legal system and the options women have. With that kind of information my friend could talk to any type of women's group.

I know another writer of "whodunits" who actually went to a body farm—a research facility where human decomposition can be studied in a variety of settings, like outside, under a building, inside a building, in a trunk, etc. The purpose is to get a better understanding of the decomposition process, which will help forensic experts develop techniques for gleaning information such as timing and circumstances of death. That was an interesting talk even though I grimaced through the whole thing!

Well, I could go on, but you get the idea. There is so much more that goes into writing than just writing.

The same is true for nonfiction. My book, *Inspire! Writing from the Soul,* is a how-to on writing in the inspirational creative nonfiction style. Naturally, I speak to groups about that technique, but other topics also came from this project.

I speak about the importance of recording our life stories for future generations. In that talk, I tell about letters, diaries, and books written by men and women centuries ago and how they've challenged me and helped shape my character.

I speak on the importance of humor and how a merry heart is good medicine. Believe me, I have plenty of funny anecdotes from my own life.

Another topic is about the "evil-editor" on every writer's shoulder while he or she is trying to write and how to get rid of that pesky nuisance.

My favorite talk from this book is my *Never Too Late* speech. I tell how I struggled for years with the sense that I started writing too late and how I overcame that lie.

So you see? The possibilities are only limited by our imaginations.

Topic Profile

I've devised a profile list to jump-start the idea process. I suggest you purchase a special notebook for this project because you will refer to it when you are writing a new presentation. The last thing you want to do is search through grocery lists and phone messages. This list is not exhaustive by any means and I'm sure you will think of more things to add to it. Following is an example of the list with a brief explanation for each point:

- ***What inspired you to write in this genre?*** Tell us about the process of finding your niche. What had you written before you decided on this genre? What made you realize this genre just felt right? Maybe you decided on this genre right off the start? Why?

- **List authors whom you admire.** Make a list of authors who write in this genre.
  - ○ **What about their writing method do you like?** Do they write in first person? Do they write in first person in one chapter and third in the next? Do they have the same theme running through each book? Do they have unbelievable sense of place? To try and uncover what it is about their style you like, I suggest you free-write. If you are not familiar with this term, it just means to write whatever comes to your mind for a set amount of time (I usually write for fifteen minutes) without stopping to think, compose, and correct. Even if the thought, "I'd sure like a cup of coffee" comes to mind write it down. Keep your pen or pencil moving forward. If you are using the computer, type without looking at the screen. The purpose for free-writing is because this practice allows things to come to light. Things that had never occurred to you. It is very cathartic. It is also a good practice when something is bothering you and you can't put your finger on it.
  - ○ **How have you applied those method aspects to your writing?** This is good information for beginning writers.
  - ○ **List their books that influenced you and why.** After you've listed a book, then free-write why that book influenced you. Add some anecdotes

about your life at the time you read these books. Maybe you were a child, or in school. I remember discovering for the first time my love for reading. It wasn't until I was an adult with five children in 1985. I started reading the *Little House* books by Laura Ingalls Wilder to the children before naptime every day. After they were tucked into their beds, I'd make a cup of coffee and devour the rest of the book. From there I went straight to Jane Austen. I love that woman's writing!

o **What did you like about those books?** For instance, I like anything Jane Austen wrote. I like her strong female characters and her obvious distain for silly women and arrogant men. Here would be another good place to free-write.

o **If and how you applied those influences in your writing?** This is good information for new writers and a graceful way to refer to your book. Simply say something like, "Jane Austen's strong female characters motivated me to do the same in my book, *In Search of Gold.*"

o **Did it work for you?** You may have tried the author's style and it was either just right, or not so good. Why or why not?

o **What did you learn from these authors?** Another good place to free-write.

o **Make a list of how this can apply to your writing and help other writers.** This is a good practice for all writers. If we are living, we should be learning.

- **Tell about your research and what you learned.** This is good for all writers. Others may be writing something along the same line.
  - ○ **What resources did you use?** Some people think research is to "Google" everything. While that is helpful, it can also give very wrong information. I read one author who set her story in England. She had vivid descriptions of a particular village. But there was a problem. This author had never been in England. I had. Her descriptions were way off and some of the things she wrote about were in another part of the country. While that isn't a big deal to most readers, it does jar those who've been there. Another author wrote about my home state and had a couple leaving their home after breakfast in a horse and buggy to have lunch with friends in another city. They made it there by noon. The problem? It takes four hours by car. Therefore, it is good to help other writers learn additional ways to research besides the Internet.
  - ○ **Tell about what worked best and what didn't.** We all benefit from the trials and errors of others.
  - ○ **What interesting things did you find?** These could be little known facts or events, an interesting person, or catastrophe.
  - ○ **Did you use this unexpected information in your story?** Another great place to refer back to your book.

- o ***Tell about the time period you researched:*** This would be interesting to writers, educators, and historians.
  - ▪ ***Relationships between the sexes, races, classes.***
  - ▪ ***Education***
  - ▪ ***Dress***
  - ▪ ***Transportation***
  - ▪ ***Language, dialect, slang***
  - ▪ ***Diet***
  - ▪ ***Culture***
  - ▪ ***Entertainment***
  - ▪ ***Work***
  - ▪ ***Government***
  - ▪ ***Politics***
  - ▪ ***Catastrophic events***
  - ▪ ***Inventions***
  - ▪ ***War***
- o ***Tell how you used this information.*** This would be a good place to read an excerpt from your book or article.
- o ***Did you travel to the place of your story's setting?*** In my research I learned that in 1850 a new route to the West had been opened. Captain R.B. Marcy served as a military escort to the emigrants in 1849. He led them on the Southern Route that went to Santa Fe, New Mexico and dropped down to Doña Ana, (now Doña Ana county). From there the wagon train followed Cooke's trail to San Diego, California. Captain Marcy only went as far as Doña Ana and then returned to Fort Smith, Arkansas. Not wanting to take the long route, he hired a guide to help him find a shorter way back. They found one through the

panhandle of Texas and southern Oklahoma. Since this was an easier and safer option, gold seekers used this trail, which later became the Butterfield Stagecoach road. I wanted to see this trail for myself. Two friends and I struck out to follow the original route as closely as we could. I found a book titled, *Marcy & the Gold Seekers*, by Grant Foreman. It was Captain Marcy's journal of his expedition. There were places in the journal where the Captain described an area by landmarks. Thank goodness, Mr. Foreman noted at the bottom of the page the town that stands there today. We had a great time exploring this route and we learned a lot! This information added believability to my story. I experienced in a small part, what the emigrants saw, felt, smelled, touched, and heard. We also visited every historical spot and museum. That alone would make a great speech that I could give to tourist businesses, travel clubs, and writers.

- ○ ***Did you research a person?*** Captain Marcy was a brave and interesting person. He'd make a fantastic topic. Very few people know about him. Besides being a captain in the army, he was an explorer and an author.

   - ▪ ***Tell us about him or her.*** I would have to be careful because the Captain did so much it would take more than an hour to do him justice. In this case, I'd have to think "movie trailer" instead of "movie." Highlight what you think your audience would be most interested in.

- **Did you shape your character after that person? How?** Another good place to highlight your book or article.
- **Did you shape your story line through your research?** My story line changed after I researched. The goals were the same, but with such rich information, my characters stayed on the trail longer than I had originally planned.

Author, Jane Kirkpatrick, writes historical novels. She suggests you tell the story of your book—why you wrote it, how you hope it might reach the audience and what you think it might have to say to contemporary lives even though it is a historical novel.

With Jane's suggestions in mind you could tell:

- **Why you wrote the book or article.** What circumstances surrounded your thoughts and decisions? My book began with our family legend about an ancestor who went to the gold fields and was killed by a claim jumper.
- **How you hope it might help the audience.** Think of how it would benefit your audience.
- **How your book/article can apply to a contemporary audience?** How can we apply the characters' experiences to our lives today? What can we learn from them?

I encourage you to fill out the Topic Profile Worksheet on the following page. For your convenience, I've listed some popular genres, but you can easily modify the worksheet according to your needs. You will find that several answers can be combined into one topic. Try and come up with enough ideas to prepare at least two different presentations.

After you have your topics, what then? Go to the next chapter and find out!

Topic Profile Worksheet

Fiction

Historicals

- What inspired you to write in this genre?
    - List authors you admire.
    - What about their writing style do you like? (free-write)
    - How have you applied that to your writing?
    - Name the books that influenced you and why. (free-write)
    - What did you like about those books?
    - How have you applied that to your writing?
    - Did it work for you?
    - What did you learn from these authors? (free-write)
    - Make a list of how this can apply to and help other writers.
- Tell about your research and what you learned.
    - What resources did you use?
    - Tell about what worked best and what didn't.
        - What interesting things did you find?
        - Did you use this unexpected information in your story?
    - Tell about the time period you researched:
        - Relationships between the sexes, races, classes
        - Education
        - Dress

- Transportation
- Language, dialect, slang
- Diet
- Culture
- Entertainment
- Work
- Government
- Politics
- Catastrophic events
- Inventions
- War
  - Tell how you used this information.
  - Did you travel to the place of your story's setting?
  - Did you research a person?
    - Tell us about him or her
    - Did you shape your character after that person? How?
    - Did you shape your story line using your research?
  - Why did you write this book/article?
  - How do you hope it might reach the audience?
  - How can your book/article apply to a contemporary audience?

Mystery/Suspense/Thriller

- What inspired you to write in this genre?
  - List authors that you admire.
  - What about their writing style do you like? (free-write)
  - How have you applied that to your writing?
  - Name the books that influenced you and why. (free-write)
  - What did you like about those books?
  - How have you applied that to your writing?

- o Did it work for you?
- o What did you learn from these authors? (free-write)
- o Make a list of what you learned from these authors and their books.
- o Make a list of how this can apply to and help other writers.
- ▪ How did you get your idea for this story? Did you:
  - o Read or hear something in the news?
  - o Revamp something that happened years ago?
  - o Rewrite a classic?
- ▪ Tell about your research and what you learned.
  - o Did you interview anyone for information to make your mystery authentic, such as a detective, forensics, medical, or law expert?
  - o How did you get in contact with them?
  - o Was it difficult to get interviews? Any advice for your listeners.
  - o What information did you gather and how did you use it in your book or article?
  - o How did you write your story?
    - ▪ Did you make a list of clues before or during your story?
    - ▪ How did you come up with red herrings?
    - ▪ What techniques did you use to create suspense?
    - ▪ What advice do you have for mystery writers?

Women's Fiction, Romance

- • What inspired you to write in this genre?
  - o List authors that you admire.

- o What about their writing style do you like? (free-write)
- o How have you applied that to your writing?
- o Name the books that influenced you and why. (free-write)
- o What did you like about those books?
- o How have you applied that to your writing?
- o Did it work for you?
- o What did you learn from these authors? (free-write)
- o Make a list of what you learned from these authors and their books.
- o Make a list of how this can apply to and help other writers.
- Why did you write this story?
- What is the story about and how can it apply to your audience?
- Is this story based on anyone you know?
- Are you showcasing an issue that is important to you?
- What were the circumstances surrounding your decision to write this piece?
- Without disclosing names, tell us about the people you based your story on and how they influenced you.
- Did you research for this story? Tell us how.

Nonfiction

Biography/Autobiography/Memoir

- What about this person inspired you to write about him/her? (free-write)
- If a memoir, why did you write the book?

- What you did you hope to accomplish by telling us his/her /your story?
- How did you research?
  - o Did you interview people? Tell us about that experience.
  - o Did you travel to the places where your subject lived and worked?
  - o Did you read letters and diaries?
- What did you learn about and from this person that can be applied to our lives or be examples of what to avoid? (free-write)
- What about their/your life do you think will help others and why?

How-To/Self Help/Informational/Inspirational

- Why did you write this book or article?
- How and when did you develop an interest in this subject?
- What has been your experience?
  - o Tell us about your "try and fail" stories, touching and humorous.
  - o Tell how you finally succeeded.
  - o Tell what your education/research taught you.
- How can this information help others?
  - o Give anecdotes about people who have taken your advice/ learned from you/ shared their results with you.
- Tell why and how this information can help those in your audience.

Reference/Academic

- Why did you write this book or article?
- What is your expertise in this area?
- Tell us about your experience.

- Give anecdotes about this subject.
- Suggest how this information should be used.
- How might this information help those in your audience?

Preparing a Speech

"It usually takes more than three weeks to prepare a good impromptu speech."~ Mark Twain

Some people dread preparing a speech more than giving one. I guess it is like writers who have no problem writing a novel, but dread the synopsis. It can be overwhelming, but if you break it down, it isn't so intimidating.

Begin by scrutinizing your topic profile and choose what you think best fits the occasion or what interests you and excites your imagination. Take time to familiarize yourself with your topic. Free-write your thoughts about the subject matter you've chosen, the "take away" you'd like your audience to receive, and the stories you want to tell. Then organize these thoughts and analyze for weak points. In the last step, you finalize by writing it out and practice presenting your talk.

Sound like a lot of trouble? It's worth it—trust me. I've known speakers who pride themselves in the ability to "wing it" and not prepare. "After all," they say, "I know my subject and besides, if I run short, I'll just take questions."

To me, that is disrespectful to the audience—the people who took their time and sometimes their money—to hear what this speaker had to say. They are there to glean information and advice to sharpen their skills and further themselves as authors.

I have listened to these speakers. It doesn't take long for them to get distracted, go on a totally irrelevant tangent and then they begin to ramble. They know they're in trouble and their words tumble in a gigantic mess while they try to walk their minds back to where they strayed off the path. After a while the audience is completely confused and has to work to understand what the heck these speakers are talking about.

Needless to say, those who wing it don't get many requests for their services. I don't want this to happen to you. It is best to write your speech and read it out loud. Edit out the weak parts, and then practice—a lot! If you do this, you and your audience will have a profitable experience.

Some speakers read their speeches from the podium. I don't recommend this because it alienates you from your audience. With your gaze glued to the paper on the podium, you will not connect with your audience, even if you occasionally look up.

It isn't a good idea to memorize your speech either. You might have a brain glitch and forget a couple of words, causing your mind to go blank.

By far it is best to practice, know your material, and carry a card with a brief outline to keep you on target.

This chapter is an easy guide to help you get your thoughts organized and a plan written down. It will be your script to practice and an outline for you to follow. After we go through the following suggestions, there is a speech outline to use for future presentations.

The Bones

A speech contains three elements: the introduction, the body, and the conclusion. Simple huh?

I like to divide my speech into time increments. Most groups and conferences give the speaker forty-five minutes to an hour. If I'm given forty-five minutes, my introduction is five minutes, the body is twenty-five, the conclusion is five, and that leaves ten minutes for question and answer. If I run over and it cuts into the time I've allotted for questions I offer to take questions after the session. If I'm given an hour, I increase the body to thirty minutes and Q&A to fifteen. If I only have thirty minutes, I cut out Q&A and offer to take questions after the session.

By breaking down a speech like this you will realize that you won't be talking that long at all. Plus, it helps you to decide how many points you should use.

Now, let's take a look at each element.

The Introduction

- In the introduction you should establish who you are and your purpose—what you will be speaking about. Give an overview of the points you will be expounding on. For example:

  "During this session about creative nonfiction writing, I will be speaking about the six elements used in this style: setting a scene, description by using the five senses, emotion, dialogue, internalization, and an 'ah-ha.'"

- As writers you know the importance of beginning with a hook. You will need to spark their interest, make them sit up and listen. Face it, the audience has a *what's in it for me attitude*, and they should. Don't disappoint them. A hook can be a quote, a funny anecdote, or an interesting fact. When speaking about using the Creative Nonfiction style of writing I ask this question for my hook:

"Like fiction, creative nonfiction engages the right brain of the reader. Let me give you an example of how powerful that is. In 1940 deer hunting was a twelve million dollar business, but because of one man and one movie in 1942, that business dropped to two million. Care to guess which man and movie?"

The Body

This consists of your main points and supporting facts, anecdotes, examples, etc. After deciding on your topic, choose three to five main points you want to make. It is best not to exceed five unless all the points are closely linked and have a natural sequence. For instance, the six elements of creative nonfiction.

The Conclusion

This part is important because people tend to remember the last thing they hear. Conclusions should be a summary of all your points and a restatement of your purpose. It is always good to have a "clincher" for the closing like a pertinent point, a quote, or maybe a challenge. Something that inspires your audience to use the information you just gave them. I call it the "Ah-Ha" because that is what you want them to say, "Ah-Ha, I've got it!"

Scrutinize

In the last chapter of this book, *And Furthermore,* I give you a list of questions to ask the person who invites you to speak or the event coordinator. If you do this you should have a good idea about the make-up of your audience. Take some time to examine your topic profile. What would fit your audience? If you've been given a theme, what would work best? Which topics gave you the most energy when you wrote about them? Can any of the topics be combined into talking points that follow an understandable sequence?

If you have been asked to speak:

Choose at least two topics that resonated with you. Something that not only gives you energy, but also something with information that would appeal to other writers and meet their needs.

If you do not have a speaking engagement on the books:

Choose two topics. One that could be given to a writers' group and one that would appeal to a "subject specific" group—where people who share the same interest gather together. For instance, while researching my novel I learned a lot about cooking on the trail. I could use that for homemaker or culinary clubs. I also grew to appreciate the bravery and self-sacrificing spirit of the women, which would make a great topic for women's groups. During my talk I can refer to my book.

Familiarize

Have some fun with your choices. Go somewhere comfortable with paper and pencil and free-write. I like to go to Barnes and Noble, get a skinny latte, and sink into a chair. They usually have jazzy music and no one bothers me. I get gloriously lost scribbling away. I may use as little as an eighth of what I've written, but that eighth is something I would have never thought of in the practical framework of my mind. Besides, I usually use the rest of my scribbles some other time.

Organize

Now it is time to organize your information. Use the outline at the end of this chapter to help with this process.

Topic:

- Decide on a working title
- Make a list of your main points

Introduction:

- Write a statement to establish you as an authority and your purpose for being there. Don't let the word "authority" throw you. It is simply a way to establish why you are there. Hopefully someone introduced you before you stood to speak and gave all your pertinent information. So when you start you can give your purpose and "restate" your expertise. For instance, let's say I'm speaking on the creative nonfiction style:

    "For the next few minutes I want to speak to you about the creative nonfiction writing style. I've been using this style for several years. From the start, I've been drawn to this style because of its powerful influence on the reader."

- Decide on your hook. Remember it could be a story, joke, quote, or a fact.
- Give a brief overview of your main points. In addition to your hook, this overview also piques the interest of your audience. It helps them to know what to expect.
- Write a transitional statement that leads into the body of your speech.

Body:

- Here you will list each point in your outline. Start with what you consider the most important point. Follow with the least important and finish with next to the most important point. The reason you want to do this is because people tend to remember the first and last points. So if your most important points are in this order: A,B,C,D, you will want to make your points in this order: A, D, C, B.

- Under each point write supportive information (anecdotes, facts, quotes, point of view). Feel free to write all that comes to your mind and all the interesting facts and quotes. You will not use everything, but in the "flow" you will discover nuggets of informative treasure.

- Following each point write a transition sentence to the next point. For instance, if I were transitioning from Dialogue to Internalization, I'd say something like:

    "Dialogue is when you are talking to others, but we also talk to ourselves, don't we. That is called internalization."

- After the final point write a transitional sentence to the conclusion. For instance:

    "By using these fiction techniques your nonfiction will not only read like a novel, but it will be remembered."

Conclusion:

- Summarize your main points. Just name them. It isn't necessary to discuss them any further. Also, this isn't a place to introduce new ideas even if they come to you at that moment. Save them for the next time.

- Restate your purpose. For instance: *"I hope this inspires you to try the creative nonfiction style of writing."*
- Write your Ah-ha. Your "value-added" zinger at the end. It can be a challenge, a quote, or simply a little something that gives hope or leaves your audience with a smile.

Analyze

Now it is time to examine your outline.
- Are your main points strong?
- Is your supporting information pertinent? Entertaining?
- Do your main points flow in sequence? In writer's jargon, do any of your main points jerk your listener out of your speech making them say, "huh?"
- Cross out anything that stops the flow of your talk.

Finalize

Rewrite your speech, word for word. Then decide if you still like the working title. If a better one comes to mind, change it. Now you have your script. Practice it! Read it out loud over and over. Walk around the house reading it to your audience of coffee tables and bathroom mirrors. Practice until you can give your speech from the outline instead of the word-for-word copy. And when you have it down pat—practice again. Use the outline on the next page to write down the bones of your talk and then flesh it out.

You have your speech, but now what? Let's go to the next chapter and find out.

Speech Outline

I. Topic

   a. Working title

   b. Main points

II. Introduction

   a. Statement to establish myself and purpose

   b. Hook

   c. Overview of main points

   d. Transition statement from introduction to body

III. Body

   a. First main point

      i. Support material (facts, anecdote, example)

      ii. Transition statement to next point

    b. Follow this pattern for subsequent points

    c. After your final point write a transitional sentence to the conclusion

IV. Conclusion

    a. Summary of main points

    b. Restatement of your purpose

    c. The "Ah Ha" close

Presenting a Speech

"Good communication does not mean that you have to speak in perfectly formed sentences and paragraphs. It isn't about slickness. Simple and clear go a long way." ~ John Kotter

I found out the hard way that a good speech presentation begins days, even weeks before I stand in front of the audience. I discovered this truth when I started speaking for Stonecroft Ministries on their circuit. Speakers for Stonecroft travel to different women's brunches and luncheons and share how a relationship with Jesus Christ has positively changed their lives.

The problem is my personality type has a tendency to improvise instead of spending time preparing. I really didn't practice much. After all, who knew about my life better than I did? I also tended to be disorganized, distracted, and I waited until the last possible minute to do anything.

I'll never forget my first time to speak at a brunch sponsored by Stonecroft. I woke up early and tried to find something to wear. Of course, nothing seemed to "work" that morning. By the time I'd chosen an outfit, not a single piece of clothing remained on the hangers. Accessorizing and finding shoes was the next challenge.

Time ticked away and the drive to my engagement was an hour away. I still had to shower, style my hair, and put on makeup. Wouldn't you know that my hair just wouldn't do a thing? My nerves were in overdrive causing me to sweat. Make-up smeared all over my face.

After throwing on my clothes, I hurried out the door and raced to the meeting. Thankfully, I arrived on time. All was well, except for one thing—I forgot my notes. Hundreds of mental bumblebees buzzed inside my head.

You know, it's surprising how one can stumble on for thirty minutes, not making one bit of sense, even though she is speaking about her life—her life that she knew better than anyone else.

You would think after that experience, I would have learned—but no. Did I mention I procrastinated? When groups, other than Stonecroft contacted me, I'd put my speech together just a couple of days before the engagement and would actually be revising only hours before I spoke. At times like those my gift of verbose prattle saved me. However, my audience, while entertained, left with nothing. That bothered me, because I knew how much I wanted good information when I attended meetings.

Those manic days prior to engagements were emotionally and physically exhausting. Things had to change, and those things were my bad habits.

There may be several insecurities between you and the microphone like fear, anxiety, questions about what to wear, what to do with your hands, whether you should move around when you talk or stand still. And, the ultimate apprehension, what if someone starts snoring in the middle of your program? (It will eventually happen.)

In this chapter I will share how to give an effective and smooth presentation with information gathered from my experiences over the years and from observing other speakers. Let's start with almost every person's primary dilemma—fear.

Conquering Fear

I read that public speaking is one of the top three fears people have. I believe it! I've seen people step back when being handed a microphone. You would think someone tried to give them a cobra. I like this quote by Jerry Seinfeld:

"According to most studies, people's number one fear is public speaking. Number two is death. Death is number two. Does that sound right? This means to the average person, if you go to a funeral, you're better off in the casket than doing the eulogy."

Most speakers have a few "flutterbys" flitting about in their stomach just before they walk up to the podium. I know I do. Sometimes adrenaline overload pumps through my body making it hard to breathe normally. However, after the first few words I connect with the audience and all fear is forgotten.

After making innumerable blunders, I've figured out it was okay to make a mistake as long as I recovered gracefully and made a little joke about my error, then continued with my presentation. Instead of panicking, I chalked it up to experience and learned from it. After all, experience is indeed the best teacher. Besides, audiences are very patient with speakers. Think about it. How many times have you attended a conference or meeting where the speaker made a mistake? Did you pull out your rotten tomatoes? Or, did you mentally help them along? Therefore, since *the audience* is patient with us, then we need to be patient with ourselves.

Stress feeds fear. Over the years I've found ways to decrease the stress level and insure that both you and the audience have a positive experience. Here is what I've learned:

Get Organized

When I am contacted to speak, the event planners usually have a topic in mind. Usually it is something they have heard me speak on before or they have read my writing.

I've found, however, that I need more information than the topic they want me to speak about. For example, it is good to ask about the demographics of the audience to determine how I should slant my presentation. If I know that the audience is primarily women, I may throw in my hot-flash story. If men are attending, I'll think of another anecdote. An audience of beginning writers would need more basic information than more experienced writers.

So you can see why it is always good to ask a little about the group before you prepare. It is also good to know the average attendance in case you decide to use handouts.

More things to ask are:

- How long you are expected to speak. Knowing this will allow you to adjust your talk.
- Will you be using a microphone? If so, what kind? If it is wireless with a battery pack, ladies will need to wear a jacket with pockets to slip the pack into, pants or a belt for the pack to be attached. Of course, I learned this the hard way (as it seems I do everything) when I wore a gauzy-type dress. The wireless mic was the kind that went over the ear and the battery pack had to be hooked to my neckline in the back. I nearly choked to death as it slid down pulling the front of my dress around my neck like a noose. Very disconcerting to say the least!
- Be sure to write down the day, time, and address while you are speaking to the contact person and repeat it. Don't assume you will

remember. When I hang up, I look up the location of the event to find the best route and how long it will take to get there.

- Give yourself plenty of time to work on your presentation, make any necessary changes, and practice. It is a good idea to designate a folder for this engagement with all the information inside.

By taking these steps you will arrive confident for your presentation.

Be Prepared

Choose what you want to wear ahead of time, including shoes and accessories. This is a real stress buster. Instead of your closet looking like a cyclone blew through and your heart beating faster with every tick of the clock, you will arrive calm and well put together. Not like the frantic woman with smudged make-up that no one could see anyway because her hair covered her face. (That would be me, as you recall.)

After you've chosen your ensemble, put it on (including shoes and jewelry) and look at yourself in a full-length mirror. Move your arms up and down. Are your clothes binding you in any way?

Ladies, does your blouse gap open? Does it come un-tucked and sag over your skirt? Bend over. Does the neckline reveal too much? If you are wearing pants, turn around and check to see if there are panty lines. (This can be very distracting)

Men, do your chest hairs escape through the neckline of your shirt or poke through the material? Does your shirt come un-tucked and drape over your belt? Do shirt buttons gap open?

Now, pretend you are at the podium and step to the side a few steps, then back a few steps, then forward. Did your shoes support you or did you stumble a bit? Were they comfortable? It is best to go for comfort. If your aching feet are sending an "*SOS*" to your brain the whole time you are speaking you will lose focus. Besides, people normally only notice speakers from their waist up.

The night before you speak, put everything you intend to take—notes, visual aids, handouts, etc.—in one place. I usually put everything in my car. If that isn't an option, put your car keys on top of your pile.

Then go get some rest!

Remember It Isn't About You

The biggest fear factor for most people is insecurity about their ability and credibility. Some worry about their appearance and feel vulnerable standing in front of people where everyone can see their self-perceived imperfections. Maybe this fear took hold in them when they were children, making the grip of angst tighter with each passing year. Some compare themselves to other people and are not able to recognize their own unique qualities. Then there are the different personality types. Some people like to stay in the background and it is harder for them to put themselves out there. Me? I love microphones! But that can also present problems, as we will discuss in *Your Speaking Style*.

Whatever causes you to tremble, remember this: your audience is there for what you can give them, not to pass judgment or critique you. They don't care if you have a double chin, a baldhead, or a big badonkadonk. (If you are not sure what that is, stand in front of a full-length mirror, turn around, and look midway down)

Actually, the audience wants you to succeed. Think about all the times you've listened to a speaker at a conference. You didn't go there to scrutinize them, did you?

Those listening to you relax when you are relaxed. If you are nervous, they are nervous for you. If you are funny, they laugh. If you act like you'd rather be anywhere but there, they will resent your wasting their time

When you stand before a group, remember that you are giving them a gift. Think about them, not yourself.

Blunders Happen

No matter who you are or how much experience you have, there will be times when a brain-fog moves in and you forget a word, mispronounce something or get tongue-tied. Even presidents, no matter how eloquent their speaking skills, stumble over their words. And *they* have teleprompters!

The important thing is what you do when you make a blunder. Do you get all flustered or do you make a little joke about yourself and continue on? Remember, if you get flustered, it makes the audience uncomfortable for you. If you laugh at yourself, the audience will laugh with you and relax. Take a deep breath, let it out, and continue with a smile on your face.

There were times after a presentation when I'd realize I had forgotten to mention a point. I would fret about it and wonder how stupid I sounded. But later on I realized the audience didn't have my notes. They had no idea I'd left something out.

All was well.

Remember to conquer fear by:

- Being organized. Have your information, directions, and your speech down pat.
- Being prepared. Make sure your clothes and accessories are laid out. Put your materials together. (I always lay my keys on top of what I

don't want to forget) Then go and get a restful night's sleep.

- Keeping the mindset that it's not about you. It's all about your audience. You are there for them and they are there for them.
- Not sweating mistakes. Make light of blunders, laugh, and move on.

Body Language

It is the weirdest thing. I'm never as aware of my hands as I am when I'm speaking. The reason it is weird is that I'm a Southern gal and we Southern gals cannot utter a word without using our hands. However, when I first started speaking, my hands kept getting in the way. As a matter of fact, there were times my whole body got in the way. I hated it when I caught myself rocking like I still had a baby on my hip—a bad habit formed while raising five kids—or when I got stuck in a repetitive hand gesture like wagging my finger to the side. Then, there were the times I looked like I was trying to strangle the microphone.

Body language speaks louder than our words and often disputes our words. If our eyebrows are knit together as we trudge to the front staring at the floor, then with a stone-faced expression say, "I'm happy to be here," the audience will know we are lying through our teeth.

On the other hand, our physical gestures can add interest and drive home a point, if used correctly. First you want to send the audience the message that you really are glad to be there and you have something to give them. Walk with purpose to the front, head up, and a smile on your face. This sends a message of confidence and credibility.

Body Movement

Stand straight and distribute your weight evenly on the balls of each foot. This will make it easy for you to step away from the podium. Yes, you must move, even if it is just a few steps. No one likes watching a stone statue unless they are in Italy. I'm not saying you need to be like a tiger pacing in a cage, frantically moving back and forth.

That said, body movement reinforces what you are saying. For instance, taking a couple of steps forward suggests the point you are making is important. Returning to your original spot means the point has been made. Moving to the side indicates you are going on to the next point. And if you are really brave and relaxed you can act out what you are describing.

I like to tell the story about my youngest son, Will, riding a frozen turkey in the bathtub when he was two years old. I waited too long to thaw the twenty-six pounder in the refrigerator and my husband, a food safety expert, shot down my idea of thawing the bird in the sink. He suggested I thaw the turkey in a bathtub full of water so that the surface would remain cold. A little later on we heard this thumping and splashing in the bathroom and ran in to find our diaperless baby on top of that frozen bird. He held on with a bear hug, pushing off one end of the tub and riding it to the other end.

While telling this story I crouch over like I'm hugging the turkey and sway forward and backward mimicking William's bucking bird rodeo. It is a funny visual for a very funny story.

Another word of advice: when you change your speaking position lead with the foot nearest the direction you are going to move. That way, you will keep your balance better than if you cross one foot over the other.

Hand Placement and Gestures

When I was a little girl, one of my favorite cartoon heroes was Popeye the Sailorman. Do you remember him? The skinny sailor with *huge* arms and hands. When I first started speaking that is exactly how I felt. I clutched my hands together like a saint about to be burned at the stake. If I stood behind the podium, I kept a death grip on it. Off stage I couldn't speak without gesturing, but on stage my hands felt like lead.

One day I decided to join Toastmasters. There I learned how hand gestures could reinforce what I'm saying. At home I practiced in the mirror until my gestures became second nature and looked easy and natural. I've never had "Popeye arms" since.

If you think about it, we use hand gestures all the time. When we describe the fish that got away, what do we do? We span our arms as far as they will reach and cup our hands. When a dog gets into our trash we make a fist and shake it in the air. (At least I do.) When our baby wants to be picked up, we open our palms and hold them down to her. Let's take a look at ways you can use gestures:

- To describe. If you are talking about height, show us. If you tell us a number that can be illustrated with one hand, hold up those fingers. When telling how big your stomach felt after Thanksgiving dinner, move your hand around an enormous imaginary belly.
- To emphasize. Making a fist shows strong emotions or determination. Raising your hands indicates enthusiasm, elation, and triumph. Holding your arms out with palms open is an invitation for giving and receiving. If you bend your arms at the elbows and shrug your

shoulders, it shows confusion, irony, or bewilderment.
- To prompt. This is a way to involve your audience. For example, I ask a question that is always answered in the affirmative and hold up my hand like I did in elementary school when I knew the answer (which wasn't often). My question is something like, "How many of you agree that rejection letters are discouraging?" Your audience will raise their hands in agreement.

Of course you won't be constantly moving your hands around. It is good to find a position for your arms and hands to return to after you make a gesture. If you are holding a microphone you might allow your other arm to relax by your side or bend the elbow with your wrist resting against your stomach, hand relaxed with your middle finger lightly touching your thumb.

Another suggestion is to watch people on television, especially in commercials. Try several different positions in front of a mirror and decide what the most comfortable position is for you to start with and return to after gesturing.

Facial Expression

Your face conveys what is inside you. If your eyebrows look like they have been pinned to your forehead, even that smile plastered on your face can't hide the fact that you are frightened to death. That will make the audience uncomfortable. A frozen face will not convey anything positive. Facial expressions, if used correctly, can be a very effective way to drive your point. Especially when using humor. I adore the comedienne Jeannie Robertson. She is a great person to study for an adept use of facial expressions. Check out her site at www.jeannierobertson.com and watch her videos.

When you are speaking, make sure your expression agrees with your subject matter. In other words, you wouldn't want to be smiling if you are talking about a bloody massacre.

Eye Contact

Have you ever been speaking with someone who refuses to make eye contact? I know a person who simply cannot make eye contact. He looks around the room or stares over my shoulder while I am speaking. The only time he will look me in the eye is when he is talking. It isn't just me. He does this to everyone. It is so bad that when he asked his daughter what she wanted for her birthday, she replied, "I want you to look at me when I talk to you."

Looking people in the eye conveys the message that you value them and are interested in what they have to say. It shows you are listening to them and creates a personal connection with whomever you are speaking. Therefore, it is important to make eye contact with your audience. It communicates sincerity and honesty.

Here is a tip on how to do this and make everyone feel you are speaking directly to him or her. When I stand before a group of people, I mentally divide the room into three sections. In each section I chose a couple of friendly faces and look them in the eyes for five seconds or less while I'm speaking. It isn't obvious to those in the audience. They all think I'm looking at them. It's kind of like those portraits in a museum where you'd swear the eyes are following you. Only this isn't as spooky.

While you speak, be sure to give each section your attention. Don't favor one side and ignore the other. That said, be natural in your movement and pause for each section. You don't want to look like an oscillating fan.

Your Speaking Voice

The first time I heard my recorded voice I swore I would never speak again. I was in kindergarten at the time. My dad's friend knew the DJ at our local radio station and he wanted me to do a tiny spot for the station. I still remember my line, "My daddy listens to KXEO 'cuz that's the thing to do!"

The DJ coached me to draw out the word "my" so I said, "Maaaaaah daddy listens to KXEO 'cuz that's the thing to do!"

When I heard the commercial, I wanted to crawl under my toy box. Even at the tender age of five, I knew I sounded like a hick on a hay wagon. Thankfully, being a child, I recovered the next day and forgot all about it.

I had a similar experience many years later when my friend, Cozy Dixon, started a ladies' Bible study at our church. She chose me and two other ladies to teach with her. The study was such a success some of the ladies suggested we tape our talks so they could pass them along to friends. It sounded like a good idea. That is until after I listened to myself. I wanted to find that toy box to crawl under.

In my mortifying "you might be a redneck" vocabulary was the word "yer" (your). I kept saying it over and over. I'm still blushing. That wasn't the only word. I also used the redneck compound words: "yousta" (used to) gonna (going to) wanna (want to), well, you get the point. All I can say is the comedian, Jeff Foxworthy, would have been proud of me.

Of all the words, "yer" bothered me the most. To add insult to injury, shortly after I heard that tape, I renewed my license plate. You will never guess what it was. "YER 283."

Somebody up there has a real sense of humor!

Most people I know do not like the sound of their recorded voices. But, if you use your voice right, it can be a part of your charm. It's like a musical instrument that you learn how to play by practicing. Here are a few suggestions to "tweak" your speaking voice:

- Watch your tempo. Some of us are slow speakers while others are speed speakers. The important thing is for us to get into a rhythm the audience can follow. If you are too slow the audience will be bored, too fast and they will be confused. A good rule of thumb is to speak the same rate as you would if you were reading out loud to someone and you wanted to be sure they heard every word.
- Enunciate. Ask a friend to help you identify the words you "wallow" in your mouth and those you run together. (Like I do.)
- Vary your pitch. Try to avoid the level, monotone voice.
- Pause. This serves many purposes. After you make a statement, a pause is like an "em" dash in your writing. It adds emphasis. This is especially useful in humor. The pause also gives your audience time to respond, and gives you time to take a deep breath or check your notes. While you practice your presentation, note good places for you to pause, like spots in your talk where you know the audience is going to respond with either laughter or draw in their breath and whisper, "Oh, no!" Also, it is fine to pause between points to give the audience time to digest what you've just said.
- Vary your volume. If you are telling about a high-speed chase, you will speak a little louder and faster. When you tell a sad story about a puppy being run over by a car, you should speak softer and slower.

- Speak conversationally. I've listened to speakers who frown and speak with such intensity, I felt like a bad little girl receiving a scolding. Those speakers may feel they are driving home an important point, but they are just plain annoying.

What to Wear

In the public-speaking world, the rule-of-thumb is to dress one step above the audience. If you are speaking at a function where the dress is casual, jeans for example, then dress business casual like slacks and collared shirt for the men, nice pants and jacket or skirt and sweater for the ladies. If the group is dressy casual, lady speakers might wear a pantsuit, skirt suit, or nice dress. Men should wear a suit and tie.

That said, I have found public speaking for writing groups and conferences are sometimes different—more casual—even among editors and agents. Most of the men I have seen wear jeans or khakis, a shirt with or without a collar and a sports coat or jacket. The women wear nice pantsuits or skirts, a blouse, and a sweater, vest, or jacket.

Some dress according to their genre. I don't think it is intentional. It's just them. Gentlemen speakers who write Westerns usually wear jeans, cotton shirt, black jacket, string tie, cowboy hat and boots. The Western ladies might wear a skirt, blouse, and a vest adorned with silver and turquoise.

I've noticed male presenters who write crime and mystery stories often wear dark colors. Ladies who write romance wear dresses and skirts made from soft flowing fabric. I think it is fun to dress the part.

My rule is to not only dress appropriately but to also dress comfortably. Make sure clothing fits and doesn't distract you from your presentation. It's frustrating to constantly be fidgeting with a neckline that keeps threatening to show all, or a tie that feels like a noose.

For one engagement I decided to wear a pair of leggings under my skirt. Why? I honestly don't know. It just seemed like a good idea at the time. When I arrived and got out of the car, the elastic waistband of the leggings had worked down to the middle of my hips, while the elastic waistband of my skirt still fit snuggly. It was miserable. I went to the ladies room and pulled up my leggings, but the whole time I spoke I could feel them slinking back down my hips. My mind raced with the fearful thought of them falling down around my knees. Honestly, how could I gracefully recover from that? Needless to say, I've never made that mistake again.

For the guys, dressing is pretty easy. Just make sure you don't look like you've slept in your clothes. Also, if you are blessed with chest hair, you might think about wearing a tee shirt underneath your shirt to stop those determined hairs that always seem to work through the fabric like weeds in a garden.

If you are going to be speaking where a spotlight is used and you are balding, apply a little face powder to avoid a distracting shine. Get a female confidante to help you with color tone.

One other thing, *always* check your pants zipper. No flashing the audience!

Dressing for the gals is a little more involved. Actually, a lot more involved. Here are a few more tips for you ladies:

- If you are speaking at a more professional event don't forget to check and see what kind of sound system you will be using. If it is a wireless headset, dress accordingly. A jacket with pockets, something with a waistband or belt will work best.

- Sheer material is not your friend in a spotlight. Stand in front of a sunny window with your legs shoulder width apart and ask a family member or friend if they can see through your clothes.
- If you wear a slip make sure it isn't too long and doesn't peek from underneath your hem. If your dress or skirt has a slit, make sure your slip is the kind with a tapered slit like a tulip slip and line it up with the slit on your outerwear.
- Skin tone bras work best under any type clothing. Even if you are wearing a white bra under a white blouse, it still shows—especially in flash pictures.
- If you have a problem with drooping bra straps, secure them together with a little piece of ribbon across your back or purchase elastic straps made for that purpose. Most department stores carry them in their lingerie areas.
- Make sure zippers work and buttons are sewn on snugly.
- Don't wear spike heels. You will thank me later.
- Huge, shiny, jangling jewelry is bothersome to you and distracting to your audience. The microphone will pick up jingling noise and the light will reflect off shiny earrings and necklaces.
- If you are speaking where a spotlight is used, take your cosmetics up a couple of notches. These lights wash out all the color in your face. You do not want to look clownish, but do go heavier on the foundation, powder, and blush. Accent your eyes with liner and shadow, and use a lip pencil to define your lips and fill in with lipstick.

After you've practiced, assembled your speaking wardrobe, practiced some more, organized, and practiced even more, the next step is to speak! But where? If you are just starting out, no one knows about you yet. No problem. I have a few ideas. Follow me to the next chapter.

Finding an Audience

"Communication is depositing a part of yourself in another person." Author Unknown

Now that you've chosen your topic, learned the basics of presenting your speech, and have practiced (a lot), you need an audience. There are many ways to accomplish this. Read through my suggestions and try a few. It is important to take that first step, even though it's uncomfortable. Speaking is easier after you've done it a few times. Especially when someone walks up to you afterwards and asks you to speak for their group.

Networking

Networking is a means of sharing information and offering your services to individuals or groups who have a common interest. This can be done in clubs, community groups, conferences, at work, or anywhere people gather who have the same interests as you. I have found this is a good way to get a speaking "gig."

For instance, at writer's conferences there are people all around you with the same passion. Their conversations cover every nuance about writing. It is easy to mention your topic and get a discussion started. Then casually mention that you speak about the subject.

Now, before the alarms go off in your head and you shout at me, "Wait, Linda! I haven't spoken about it yet!"

Yes. You have

You've given your speech time and time again to the furniture, the cat, dog, fish—whatever—not to mention the audience in your mirror.

You have practiced haven't you?

Don't limit yourself to networking strictly in writing groups. Network any time you attend a gathering of people who share a common interest in your topic. Have your networking tools—business cards—with you at all times. We will discuss those and other tools at the end of this chapter.

My dear friend, Lois Spoon, successfully fought breast cancer for many years. She wrote about her experiences and spoke to cancer support groups, support groups for family and friends of cancer victims, and several ladies' banquets. She bravely finished her battle in 2002, however, her impact lives on.

I sold a story to *Chicken Soup for the Soul Mothers of Preschoolers*. I wrote about how I had lost "me" while raising five children and realized I needed to take care of myself as well. This would be a good topic for *MOPS* (Mothers of Preschoolers), homeschool support groups, and any local parenting group.

Remember the story I mentioned about my toddler riding the frozen turkey in the bathtub? I used it for my topic at a ladies' Christmas banquet as a humorous presentation. I'm still getting positive comments on that one. In fact, I've been asked to speak at their women's retreat.

Attend Events

Attending events where the interest relates to your book in some way might provide people who might be interested in your speaking to their group.

The annual Books in Bloom event takes place every May in Eureka Springs, Arkansas, bringing together accomplished authors, booklovers, and writers. It is a free literary festival, presented by the Carroll and Madison Public Library Foundation that is open to the public and celebrates book culture and promotes reading and literacy.

Bring your business cards and network. These affairs happen all over the country. Search the Internet for "book events" in areas within driving distance near you.

Another good example of attending events is my colleague, Nita Beshear. She wrote a devotional book, *Devoted to Quilting,* published by Devoted Books. Nita attends quilt shows to sell books and network with other quilters and crafters. She has a lot to offer crafting groups and clubs as well as writers' groups.

Do Your Research

Take a look at your topics and see what group would be a good fit. Again, do an Internet search on the different groups, clubs, and associations that meet close to where you live. Check with the local Chamber of Commerce's website to see what organizations are in your area. Look up "Associations" in the phone book and any business that might correspond with your topic. Don't forget schools, Parent-Teacher Associations, and the Scouts. Look in the "Society Page" or "Club Briefs" section of your local paper to see what clubs, societies, and associations meet nearby. If any make a good match with your topic, get in touch with them by either calling the contact person or sending your *one-sheet*. What's a one-sheet? I'll tell you about it in the *Tools to Have on Hand* section later on.

As I mentioned earlier, I'm writing a novel about a young woman who is trying to find her father on the goldfields during the 1850 Gold Rush. I used the topic profile and made a list of possible topics. Listed below are a few potential topics and groups that might be interested in them.

- Women in the Gold Rush. This topic is full of possibilities.
  - ○ I could highlight a particular woman.
  - ○ I might address the many cultural differences of those on the trail. People from all over the world came to find gold. During their travels they interacted with Indian and Mexican women. The trail was a great equalizer.
  - ○ I could speak about their example of unmatched bravery and self-sacrifice. These women had no choice but to go when their husbands said, "Go." They left their families, comfortable homes, and social circles to travel among strangers, sleep in tents, and give birth in wagons where everyone could hear their cries. Women lost their children to disease and accidents. They buried their loved ones by the side of the road, never to return. This subject would be interesting to historical societies, any women's civic group, club, or ministry, library programs, school programs, and of course, writing groups.
- Medical practices on the trail.

  In addition to the crude compounds mixed by doctors and druggists, the travelers depended on herbal remedies. This would be of interest to garden clubs, any group espousing holistic or natural health, historical societies, or schools. I might even bring an example of some of the herbs.

- Food on the trail.

Cooking on the trail presented many challenges to the women who left well-appointed kitchens. Such as making biscuits, pies, and cakes over an open fire. Variety presented another problem. Halfway through the journey their food supply was depleted leaving only sparse ingredients like flour, side meat, and potatoes. Therefore, they had to find local provisions to add variety and create satisfying meals. Some fried up a platter of "bush-trout" or in other words, rattlesnake. Indeed, they were very inventive. Any culinary club, homemaker's club, or school would like this topic. Especially if I demonstrated one of the recipes. (Forget the rattlesnake!)

- Relationships on the trail.

Death, an unwelcomed visitor, frequented those on the trail. Widowers needed help with their children. Widows needed the protection and provision only a man could provide. This made for rushed and unromantic unions. Women bonded with other women, because, frankly no one else could understand their anger, fear, pain, and weariness. Any women's group, historical group, or school might welcome this topic.

Ask Your Friends

Friends and colleagues who are speakers may be willing to help you. Remember my friend, Dusty Richards? He's a big cowboy to whom you say, "Yes, Sir." He has pushed me through many doors I wouldn't have peeked through on my own. Dusty knows me and has heard me speak. I'm not afraid to ask him to recommend me. However, when I am given an opportunity from one of Dusty's recommendations, I am very careful to be responsible. I arrive on time and am cordial, because it is his reputation as well as my own that is on the line.

Writers' Groups

I belong to the Northwest Arkansas Writers, a critique group. We meet every Thursday night to read our works-in-progress to the group. We offer suggestions on how to make each piece stronger. Most of us were unpublished when we joined. Now most of us *are* published. Critique groups make a big difference. If there is a writers' critique group in your area, check it out. These groups network with other groups. When a speaker is needed, members of the group are recommended based on the topic and need. Our group conducts a free full-day workshop every March. Our numbers grow each year and we often contact people from other groups to speak.

Listservs

A listserv is an e-mail discussion on a particular subject. I belong to several. You interact with people from all over the world. Yahoo Groups and Google Groups are a good place to start. Look at their directories and choose groups that look interesting and focus on your subjects and type of writing. This is a great way to share your knowledge, learn something new, get your name out there and connect with other writers.

Social Networks

A social network is another way to connect with friends and people who share your interests. Facebook, Myspace, and many others offer a place to post your work, thoughts, and speaking information. They are free and you only give the information you are comfortable posting.

I have a Facebook account and decided to start a group called, *Inspire with Linda Apple*. Each Monday I choose a quote and apply it to daily life as a means to motivate and inspire. It has been rewarding to receive emails from members of my group and others I've never met, expressing how the message was exactly what they needed.

Another benefit I really didn't expect is the enthusiastic response. Pastors are using my little inspirations as sermon illustrations and posting them on their church blogs. People are mailing them to their friends and sharing my link. Every day more and more people are joining. It is spreading at a dizzying speed. Just goes to show you how many people need a good word.

Here I'm accomplishing two things: encouraging others and posting an example of my work and what I'm all about.

Business-Oriented Social Networks

Linkedin is a good site to join after you gain experience as a speaker and want to pursue it further, because it opens doors for you in the business community. When event planners need to hire someone, they usually search these sites. You can also ask those who have heard you speak to give you a recommendation.

Blog

A blog is a "web log." It's free and easy to set up. In fact, many people use a blog for a website. Choose a title that reflects your interests and post often. I have three. One for inspiration called Linda C Apple—www.lindacapple.blogspot.com, one for new writers, Daydreaming on Paper—www.daydreamingonpaper.blogspot.com, and a travel blog, This Southern Gal's View of the World—www.southerngalsview.blogspot.com.

I've enjoyed hearing from readers all over the world. Not only will this give you a great place to showcase your work, you just might get an invitation to speak. I haven't yet, but I keep hoping someone in the UK will ask me to speak—all expenses paid, of course.

It is a good idea to read other people's blogs and follow the ones you like. Be sure to leave intelligent comments. You never know who will read it and check out your blog. Make sure you include your "speaker" info and your contact information.

Ezines

Online magazines sometimes accept work from freelance writers. Do a search on ezine directories and check out ones that fit with your topics. Check to see if the ezine publishers uses freelance writers and if they do, send them a query. Ezines and ebooks are the future, and thousands of people already read them. Therefore, this is another great way to get your name and your topic in front of people.

Volunteer at Local Schools

My friend, Jeanie Horn, author of *Saucier's Meadow*, volunteered at the local elementary school to read to the children. She wore jeans, a bright western shirt, boots, and a hat with a long feather. The kids were as mesmerized with that feather as with her reading. Jeannie sat on the floor so she could be eye-level with the children as she read, then she asked questions. The children's responses were enthusiastic, as well as the teachers'.

Encouraged by her success with the students, she began conducting writing workshops for them and sponsored a writing contest. Soon the high school contacted her to do the same for them.

My grandson, Ethan, told his teacher that his Nonni (me) was a writer. She invited me to speak to the kids. What fun we had. I took a stuffed pink flamingo and we wrote a story about him on the board. The kids waved their hands eager to share their great ideas. Afterwards, I received more invitations at local schools. Best of all, I saw the pride in my grandson's eyes.

Most schools welcome volunteers. If you have a child or grandchild in a local school, volunteer to read, tell stories, or talk to the students about what it is like being an author. Teachers may want you to work along with them to reinforce something they are teaching.

If you do not have a child in a local school or a contact who can vouch for you, call the school administration office and ask to speak with the person who handles public relations. Tell the PR person who you are, what you write, and what you can offer as a volunteer in the local schools. Most educators are open to programs that further their students' interest in reading and writing.

There are many more clubs and organizations for you to approach in order to get your name and work in front of people. It will take time to seek them out and you may come to a lot of dead ends, but then again, you may strike gold.

One speaking engagement often leads to another. When the opportunity presents itself, don't be afraid to offer your speaking services. The worst anyone can say is, "No." After all, you *are* a writer and if you submit, then you are probably used to rejection. And what do we do when we are rejected? We resubmit somewhere else.

Tools to Have on Hand

Business Cards

As you may know, when writers get together this question will always be asked, "Do you have a card?" If you do not have cards, I suggest you buy some. It is much more professional to whip out your card rather than to sheepishly admitting you don't have one and scrounging for a scrap of paper to write down your information.

There are many options available. You can use the business card template on your computer or search "business card templates" on the Internet. Office stores and discount stores such as Walmart have business card sheets that tear with clean lines in the office supply department. I suggest you stay away from the perforated ones because they leave a ragged edge.

For a more professional look go to Vista Print (www.vistaprint.com). This company offers free cards, charging only for shipping. Their one stipulation is to be allowed to put their company logo on the back of the card in the lower left corner. They also offer premium cards at a reasonable price, with the advantage of making them more personal.

There are different schools of thought regarding what to have on your card. I have my name, address, phone number, email, website, and blog sites. Some feel having the address and phone number compromises their safety, but most of us have this information in the phone book anyway. However, if you are uncomfortable giving out your home address and phone number just use your name and email. I also recommend putting your photo on the card. I once had another writer challenge me on this, saying it appeared *amateurish*. But common sense tells me that if I give my card to someone at a conference, even after a few weeks this person will remember me — much more than those who gave out a card with just their name.

Promotional Sheets

This is a personal promotional sheet also known as a *one-sheet*. It is a quick synopsis of who you are and what you do. Think of it as a snapshot, rather than a movie.

For those who hate "cold-calls," this is a handy tool because you can simply mail your sheet to places where you'd like to speak. These are also good for placing on the "freebie" table at conferences or sending to anyone who has contacted you about speaking for their group.

Keep it succinct and make every word count.

Your one-sheet should include:
- Contact information, including your website and blog site. These give event coordinators a feel for your personality and your writing. It will help them to decide if you are a good fit.

- Your photo. It is best if this is professionally done. Not necessarily a stiff headshot, but one reflecting your personality.
- Your tagline. This is known as *branding*. It is a one-line summary of who you are and what you do. It shows your unique niche and what makes you different from everyone else. You have probably seen these on websites. My tagline is *"Inspiring Lives through Voice and Pen"* because my focus is on inspiring others and I do this through speaking and writing. Velda Brotherton writes historical fiction and nonfiction. Her brand is *"Stories Woven in Time."*
- A brief biography that establishes your credibility and your qualifications to speak on this subject. Highlight your expertise and life-story as it applies to your book and is relevant to your audience's interests.
- Your topics. Give an overview of your topic in a couple of lines and also tell what the audience would gain from your presentation.
- Your standard topics. If you have developed workshops or training classes, be sure to add them to your one-sheet. Write a two or three line description and bullet point the benefits your audience will receive. Also note that you can customize your presentation according to their needs.
- Testimonials. Usually, after you speak, several people will want to meet you and tell you how they enjoyed your talk. Make note of some of their comments and add them to your sheet. Also ask the person who invited you if he or she would write a letter of recommendation for you to add to your sheet.

The layout of your one-sheet is almost as important as your information. If possible, it is best to have it professionally designed and printed on glossy 48 lb paper. However, if this isn't an option for you, then use software such as Microsoft Publisher, and choose one of their templates for a flyer. You can also search the Internet for "free templates for flyers."

I have a few suggestions for the layout:

- Have your name across the top in large font.
- Put your picture on the top right or top left beside your name or just under it.
- Use glossy, white paper. This gives a professional appearance and provides the best pallet for your information and your photograph. Let the ink be your color.
- Use black ink for your main text and no more that two colors for any other text you might want to add. Make sure if you decide to shade a textbox with a background color that your text is easy to read. For instance, if you use dark purple for your background you wouldn't want to use black ink for your text.
- Bold your contact information.
- Good titles to use for your testimonials are *Testimonials, Audience Comments, What people are saying about* _____.
- For good visual examples do an Internet search by typing in "speaker one-sheet."

Promotional Packs for Advanced Speakers

For those of you who realize you actually enjoy speaking, I suggest investing in a promo-pack. These can be pricey to put together so don't go overboard. I usually make ten at a time.

Take a few with you when speaking or while attending a writing conference or any other similar event. Then, if someone expresses an interest in your speaking for their conference or large event, you will have the promotional packs handy. If there is a conference or event where you want to speak, these packs are what you would mail to the contact person.

Your promotional pack should include:

- A CD of you speaking, preferably in front of an audience. You will be more natural that way. If no one is recording at the event, ask a friend to record you on a digital recorder. If the place where you are speaking is making a DVD, be sure and ask for a copy.
- Your one-sheet. If you are sending it to a particular event or group, make sure your one-sheet relates to their needs. Choose topics you would like to present at their event and include an outline of that presentation.
- Your business card.
- Letters of recommendation. Ask past event planners you've spoken for to write one for you. If you have received letters from past audience members include one or two.
- Your fee schedule. We will discuss how to determine this at the end of this chapter.
- Articles that have been published about you. Don't forget any ezine articles.
- A copy of your book. If the conference could make a lot of important contacts or a large fee, then it worth the expense to include your book. If it isn't a large event, send a jpeg of your book cover. For those who have articles in magazines send a sample copy.

Purchase presentation folders at your local business store to hold the above items. Choose the ones with slits on the inside flap for your business card. Some business stores offer custom folders. You might want to check that out.

Setting a Fee Schedule

You will find different suggestions on how much to charge for your speaking services. But since I'm focusing on writers, I will tell you about my experience. When I first started I mostly spoke to small writing groups. I considered the experience and exposure as fee enough. After all, if I blew it, they weren't out any money. If I had to travel out of town, they always covered my expenses. There were times I even received a small honorarium.

As I gained more experience I received honorariums to my satisfaction making it easy for me to avoid setting a fee schedule. But there comes a time when it must be done. I have found a speaker is more respected when the group pays a fee. The higher the charge, the more a speaker is valued. Strange, huh?

However, I am very flexible. Most groups have limited funds and since I love what I do, I will work with them. My first priority is to help other writers achieve their dreams, which also advertises my work and builds my platform.

Conferences usually have larger budgets and it is important to know what you want to charge in this case. The following are suggestions for you to build upon.

- Beginner speaker-Those who have only spoken locally and are either yet-to-be published, published locally, or self-published only. While you are getting your "speaker-legs" consider the experience your payment. Right now you are casting about trying to find a place to speak, and if you do well, word will spread. If you struggle a bit during your talk, then no money is lost. As you get more experience and confidence you will probably be offered an honorarium when you are invited to speak.

This could be from $50.00 - $250.00. If you are asked what you charge, make sure your fee matches your confidence. If you say $250.00 and then give a $2.00 program, word will get around.

- Intermediate speaker-Those who have spoken regionally (multi-state) and have been published multiple times or have at least one published book. Again, this depends on your experience and your program. If you've received emails and letters from former audience members who've told how much you've helped them, then charge accordingly. You have been proven. Depending on budget concerns I suggest a range of $300.00 - $600.00 per session. For conferences you may want to charge more.

- Accelerated Intermediate speaker-Those who have spoken regionally, have good name recognition, and a following in addition to several published books. You will be able to ask for a higher fee. And, like I said earlier, the more they pay the more they value you as a speaker. I suggest a range from $300.00 to as much as $1,200.00

- Advanced speaker–Those who have several books published, have a solid national following, and high name recognition. These speakers usually start at $2,500.00 and can command up to five and six figures. (Must be nice!)

Again, this is only a guide to help you in considering what to charge. Time and experience help clarify what you should charge. One thing to remember, fee or no fee, **always** request that your expenses be covered. This covers transportation costs (gas, airfare), meals, and your hotel room.

The next chapter will not only help you develop as a speaker, it will also help you understand yourself and others better. If you are already speaking you will recognize your speaker strengths and how to develop them even more. You will also identify your speaker weaknesses and how to overcome them. If you haven't started speaking, this will help you know what to watch out for.

Interested? Turn the page and let's take a look.

Your Speaking Style

"In other living creatures the ignorance of themselves is nature, but in men it is a vice."~ Boethius

We all are unique in our own way, and yet, some of us are curiously similar. I understood why after I read Tim LaHaye's book, *Spirit Controlled Temperaments,* many years ago. The premise of his book is based on Aristotle's theory and subsequent teaching that our temperament (our natural predisposition) is based on the predominance of one (or a blend) of the four humours (body fluids) in the human body: Yellow Bile, Black Bile, Phlegm, and Blood.

Aristotle thought the dominance of yellow bile caused a person to be choleric making them passionate, ambitious, energetic, domineering, quick-tempered, and impatient. A dominance of black bile produced a melancholic person resulting in a creative, deep, kind, depressed, negative, and skeptical temperament. Phlegm dominance brought about a phlegmatic person manifesting as a personality that was content, calm, rational, slow, shy, and unemotional. Blood dominance made people sanguine causing them extroverted, friendly, social, forgetful, unorganized, and chronically late.

Before Aristotle, Hippocrates believed when one fluid was dominant over the others an imbalance resulted causing disease. Empedocles paired the four universal elements of nature—earth, fire, water, and air—with each fluid: earth with black bile, air with blood, fire with yellow bile, and water with phlegm.

Many personality profiles have come from these ancient teachings. They are designed in many ways: four animals, four colors, four numbers and letters, four universal elements or the four humours. Whatever the profile, they always use four types and their blends because it is rare that anyone can be described as solely one type. Usually a person is combination of two dominant types. It is amazing how accurate all of these profiles are and how easily we can identify ourselves.

All of the profiles essentially reach the same conclusions and we usually do not have a hard time recognizing ourselves in all of them. However, I prefer Laurie Beth Jone's use of the attributes of nature in her book, *The Four Elements of Success*, for personality sketching.

Nature is easy to recognize and is the only format that gives us a visual picture of how the different characters of each personality blends in us and how our temperament interacts with the temperaments of others. Therefore, for clarity's sake, I am going to use the universal elements of nature to distinguish the different speaking styles.

Before I do this, let me clear up a few misconceptions people have:

- The purpose of these profiles is not to "label" people or limit them in any way.
- Using them in this manner is not a form of pagan worship. It is a simple, visual tool familiar to all of us, in order to enhance effective communication and promote appreciation and co-operation among people.

Distinguishing behavior traits is valuable for those of you who are currently speaking. My goal is for you to recognize your strengths and find ways to make them more effective, and also to identify your weaknesses so you can find solutions to overcome them.

If you haven't started speaking, you will determine your potential strengths and be forewarned about the possible weaknesses you should guard against.

In this chapter we will:

- Review each universal element
- Pair behavior traits associated with that element
- Identify speaker strengths and weaknesses
- Review the strengths to build upon and weaknesses to overcome.

In Florence Littauer's book, *Personality Plus*, she warns that our positives taken to extreme could actually become negatives. Therefore, after examining each element we will also look at how certain strengths could actually become weaknesses.

In this chapter, not only will you recognize your own tendencies, but you might also think of friends and family who fit each description. I hope this information will also inspire you to be patient with the oddities of others.

Air

Air—a mixture of nitrogen and oxygen that circles the earth and makes up our atmosphere. All forms of life depend on it for survival.

Air touches us. When I visit my relatives in the Deep South, we sit on the porch during the hot summer nights. Moisture-laden air settles on my skin like a wet blanket. My grandmother calls the air "close." I call it *smothering!* On the other hand, I love spring's warm evening breeze caressing my face with its velvety softness. Not so much winter's harsh wind that scrubs my cheeks and bites my nose.

Air is invisible. It blows by suddenly and then is gone. No one can predict when a gust will come or knows where it goes. But we can feel its direction and witness its effect around us. It moves things forward, like a sailboat zigzagging in the bay. It lifts up. Have you ever watched an autumn leaf twirl to the ground only to be picked up by a breeze, tossed up to fall again? But air isn't always playful. It can also be destructive. We've all seen pictures on the evening news showing entire towns flattened by tornadoes.

Air resonates and we hear its music when the wind's soft tune whistles through tree branches and rustles the leaves. Air's voice isn't always pleasant. It also moans like a haunting spirit and screams in a cacophony of voices. I've read of how many pioneer women went insane during the long winter blizzards on the prairie.

Air carries scents. I look forward to the fresh breath of spring. Have you ever caught a whiff of rain in the wind before there is even a dark cloud in the sky? How I love the fragrance of honeysuckle in the night air. In the fall, wafts of air give the faint hint of leaves burning somewhere in the neighborhood. Air sends the scent of warning to animals that impending danger is close by.

Air incorporated in certain foods make them taste better. It turns ordinary cream into fluffy whipped cream. It helps change sugar into cotton candy and egg whites into meringue.

All the senses are delighted by air, and at times, devastated by it.

So what does this tell us about air? It:

- Surrounds the earth and creates the atmosphere
- Sustains life
- Touches us
- Is invisible and unpredictable
- Can be playful
- Can be destructive
- Carries sound
- Carries fragrances and announces what is coming or impending danger
- Enhances the flavor and texture of the foods it incorporates.

Behavior Traits Associated with Air

People who have the behavior traits of air are like a breeze touching everyone around them with a gentle pat or affectionate squeeze. Air people are expressive and enthusiastic. They are kind and friendly, a breath of fresh air. They love people and have a natural gift for making everyone feel welcomed and special. At a social gathering they tend to be the center of attention because of their playful sense of humor, their loud voice, and infectious laugher.

No one can beat them at storytelling. They are masters at embellishing and adding color to an otherwise ordinary story. They just plain like to talk— and talk, and talk. It doesn't matter if they know you or not, because they have never met a stranger. Take my brother, Claude, for instance. We can be walking to my car in a parking lot and a man—total stranger, mind you—walks past us. Claude will speak and then strike up a conversation. By the time they are through talking, they are slapping each other on the back and promising to get together sometime. Amazing.

Air people are motivators and move others forward. They have the ability to improve the mood and the flavor of any occasion. That said, they can also be the most *annoying* people at a gathering when they get caught up in telling long detailed stories with the loudest voice in the room, of course. They want to be sure everyone can hear. Being caught up in their own cleverness, suddenly *it's all about them.*

They are optimistic and love change. Travel is one of their greatest passions because they are curious by nature and like experiencing different countries and cultures. If they could, they would circle the earth—just like the air.

On the down side, they get bored easily. Even though they are the masters of fun, great ideas, and starting projects, when anything ceases to be fun, they quit. If you were to peek in their junk closets you would probably find dozens of half-finished projects.

Forget organization. Their desks, closets, drawers, cars—actually, all spaces they occupy—appear as if a whirlwind blew through. They try to have some semblance of organization by stacking piles all over the house.

Air people over-commit because they hate to disappoint, but then they forget. However, their forgetfulness sometimes works in their favor because they do not hold grudges.

They are terrible time managers and are chronically late. Why? Because their minds wander, they lose focus and all sense of time. If they are cleaning a closet and a magazine or photo album happens to be there, the closet will never get cleaned. At the end of the day, you will find the air person, amid the old clothes and stacks of shoes, thumbing through the pages.

Does this sound like you? If so, read about your speaker strengths and weaknesses.

Air Speaker Strengths

Although air speakers cannot sustain life, they can certainly sustain a lively speech. They are animated, up-front people who have never been intimidated by a microphone. The world, as the cliché goes, is their stage. Like the wind, they tend to move about the platform while enthusiastically gesturing. Because of their knack for storytelling, they are masters at voice inflection as well as knowing when to include a pause in order to add punch to their humor or drama. One thing is for sure; their audience is never bored.

Being "people-persons," air speakers like to meet, greet, and mingle with people before the meeting, trying to learn their names and all the while are praying they can remember a few of those names to use during the presentation. Good eyesight and nametags are their salvation!

When air people speak they project a positive, comfortable atmosphere. Natural motivators, they move people forward to action. The sound of their voice is like that of a friend. Just as the breeze carries the fragrance of a rose or the smell of smoke warning of a fire, the air speaker brings a message of hope and counsel.

Afterwards, don't be surprised if they hang on to your hand after you've finished shaking theirs. It is second nature for them to touch while visiting.

All in all, air speakers' presentations are fun, memorable, and inspirational. Their listeners leave with a smile on their face and in their heart. Because of the air speaker's ability to create trust, the audience members will remember the information they've heard and will use it to improve their lives. A big bonus for the air speaker is that the audience members will want to hear this speaker again and will recommend him or her to other events.

Air Speaker Weaknesses

Since air speakers have this love affair with microphones and being "on" at all times, they can be overbearing and plainly put, big bores. They think their stories are so interesting that they go into waaaaay too much description, use too many details, and "color" their anecdotes (some call it exaggerating) to the point of lying. These speakers also have a tendency to give too much personal information. Since they are so trusting, their lives are an open book.

Because of their problem in maintaining focus, they tend to ramble. And while the "air" people enjoy this, others, like my husband, grit their teeth and grumble, "get to the point, already!" Another reason they rattle on is they tend to be very disorganized. Their desks look like Bourbon Street the day after Mardi Gras. Their verbal tangent is the result of poor preparation. Instead, they prefer to "wing it"—just get up there and say whatever comes to mind. The reason? They are easily bored, hate routine, (like practicing) and ignore deadlines—except for the last minute when they throw everything together!

They may think their gift of gab means they do not have to prepare and practice, but their audience will think differently. Trying to follow the rambling air speaker is literally *chasing the wind!* They don't know where the speaker is going or if they ever arrive.

Air speakers thrive on audience response. If the audience is unresponsive this will suck all the oxygen out of the air and the speaker will fall flat. They seek approval and thrive on affirmation. It is easy for them to inadvertently make everything "all about them."

Strengths to Build Upon:
- Natural movements, animated expressions and gestures. Lean into your audience and break down any invisible barriers.
- Interesting voice inflection that matches your topic. Use pauses to alert your audience that something important, or the punch line, is coming.
- Tell anecdotes relating to your point. Keep them short and tight.
- Create a warm and welcoming atmosphere. Keep your voice tone friendly and conversational.
- Mingle and learn names. Jot down the ones you want to use in your presentation.
- Motivate and inspire.

Weaknesses to Avoid:
- Adding too many details, giving too much personal information, and exaggerating to the point of lying.
- Boring the audience with a long detailed story. Keep a sharp eye on your listeners. If they are checking their watches, staring at the floor or ceiling, or covering their face with their hands it is time to move on.
- Rambling. Focus! Organize! Practice! Even if it is boring. Find a way to make it fun. You are good at that.

When Strengths Become Weaknesses:
- Animation. Don't pace the stage to the point of looking like a duck in a shooting gallery. Make

sure your gestures don't make you look like said duck is trying to fly away.

- Voice. Don't talk too loud or too fast.
- Storytelling. Don't bore your audience with a lengthy, detailed, anecdote.
- People skills. Remember to *listen* to the person you are speaking with. Don't be formulating your next sentence.
- Be sensitive. Does the person you're talking with back away or withdraw when you touch him or her? Maybe this individual feels like you are invading his or her "personal space" and doesn't like being touched. Others may welcome your hand on their arm or shoulder.

Remember:

- In addition to building your platform, you are on the stage to share information, encourage, and help your audience.
- It isn't always about us; it is also about our audience.
- The brain can only absorb what the seat can endure. If you go too long you will lose your audience. Leave them wanting more.
- If your audience is unresponsive, don't get blown away. Power through. You never know the real reason. Some could be so interested in what you are saying they are trying to get every point. Others may have stayed up with a sick loved one all night, or may be in the middle of some kind of personal conflict.

Fire

A fire's flame is hot, colorful, and mesmerizing. Anytime I enter a room with a fire in the hearth, it immediately grabs my attention. A dancing blaze on a cold winter day creates a cozy, comfortable, and inviting ambiance. We enjoy gathering around the fireplace or a bonfire and talking while savoring its warmth and beauty.

Fire illuminates. When our power is knocked out by an evening storm, we stumble around in the dark looking for matches and a candle. With the strike of a tiny match the darkness shrinks away as the flame lights the way.

Fire communicates. I have flares in my emergency kit to use if I'm stranded on the side of the road. They are also used to warn of danger ahead. When hikers lose their way or people are stranded they build fires to signal rescue crews that they are alive and where to find them.

Fire is dependent on fuel and oxygen. We can't see the oxygen it consumes nor do we pay much attention to the wood it is feeding upon because we are hypnotized by its glorious blaze.

It protects us. Fire keeps wild animals away when we are on their turf. We use fire to cook our food, killing bacteria and parasites that lurk upon the surface and within.

You could say that in a controlled setting, fire civilizes us. However, fire uncontrolled is destructive. The hungry, consuming blaze rushes forward, spreading over thousands of acres sucking all the oxygen into its flames and creating firestorms. The intense heat melts glass. And yet, for all its fury, when it has consumed all the available fuel, the fire dies.

What does this tell us about fire? It:

- Is beautiful

- Mesmerizes
- Is inviting
- Commands attention
- Illuminates the darkness
- Communicates messages
- Is dependent on other things to exist
- Protects
- Is destructive when uncontrolled

Behavior Traits Associated with Fire

People who have the behavior traits of fire are bigger than life. They command attention and at first, they fascinate people. If they are not the center of attention they will do something to be sure they are.

Fire people are bright and intelligent. We can trust what they say because they are usually right. And they are very aware they are right, only they wouldn't say "usually," they would say "always." The fire people I know are right even when they are wrong. Whatever the situation, if it goes right it is because of them. If it goes wrong it's never their fault (even though it is) but the fault of adverse circumstances or other people.

Fire people are courageous. There isn't a subject, situation, or emergency that intimidates them. They enjoy challenges—thrive on them, actually. No matter how controversial, they will move forward in places or circumstances no one else would dare approach.

They excel in emergencies. If you are ever in a catastrophic situation you will definitely want a fire person at the helm. They are clear-headed, quick thinkers, and good decision makers. Fire people know exactly what to do and we feel safe with them.

They have no need for intimate friends. However, they do enjoy people—people are their fuel. They need the accolades, compliments, and affirmations others can give. They also like to assign tasks to others. Fire people are the brains and delegators; people are their "worker bees."

Fire people are passionate, goal and production-oriented, fast movers, and strong leaders. They are succinct and get to the point without unnecessary explanations or descriptions. Just the facts, thank you very much!

They can be warm people, good conversationalists, and interesting as long as they are in the hearth, so to speak. But when out of control, they burn with their anger, consume people by placing too many demands on them, and destroy with their words. All the while, fire people cannot figure out why no one likes them because they do not realize how insensitive they can be.

Fire Speaker Strengths

Fire speakers are captivating on stage. Their confident manner inspires their audience to trust them. They are passionate in their delivery and extremely motivating. They identify problems and give solutions. Their bullet point presentations and lack of rambling is appreciated by most in the audience. Fire people are incapable of rambling. Their focus is laser sharp and they are *always* prepared. A responsive audience improves fire speakers. It is the oxygen they need to blaze brighter.

They have powerful presentations and strong voices. Every gesture is strong and purposeful. In a word, they are intense. If they are writing on a white board they will underline the word they want to emphasize four times when once would suffice.

After the presentation the audience is more than satisfied with the valuable and succinct information they've received. It has been worth their time to listen to the fire speaker.

Fire Speaker Weaknesses

The intensity and passion of this type speaker sometimes crosses the line of control. They are so into their topic that they frown and glare at the audience. They punch their finger in the air. Their voice is loud and scolding. Every now and then they pause, clutch the podium and stare into the crowd to let what they just said sink in. It wouldn't be so bad if this happened once, but their intensity self-feeds and they grow more and more fierce. If the audience members had tails, those tails would be tucked between their legs.

Since fire people have little-to-no patience with those who do not know as much as they do, they can be condescending. I've seen this happen way too many times. Should someone ask a question they consider ignorant, they may smirk, roll their eyes, shake their head, or give a cocky reply.

If they—heaven forbid—misspeak, or make a mistake, they will go to ridiculous lengths to cover it up instead of admitting it. In this case one could say that is their only form of rambling. And it is at this juncture where they lose the confidence of the audience. It simply doesn't occur to them they are that obvious.

Finally, if the audience is unresponsive, their blaze dies. Their natural inclination is to blame the audience and they might actually start berating them.

Strengths to Build Upon:
- Your ability to motivate.
- The clarity and relevance of your points.
- Building confidence and connecting with your audience.
- Preparing a dynamic program.

Weaknesses to Avoid:
- Being too intense.

- Forgetting to be sensitive.
- Being condescending.
- Trying to cover up a mistake.
- Getting frustrated with unresponsive audiences.

When Strengths Become Weaknesses:

- Make sure your passion doesn't come off as anger.
- In your efforts to help your audience understand your point be careful to avoid a condescending attitude.
- Don't let your "tight" presentation become cold and impersonal. Be sure to sprinkle a few anecdotes in your speech.

Remember:

- Speak to your audience with the same respect, voice, and tone you expect others to use with you.
- You are there for them.
- If your audience is unresponsive, don't flame out. Power through. You never know the real reason. Some may be so interested in what you are saying they are trying to get every point. Others may have stayed up with a sick loved one all night, or may be in the middle of some kind of personal conflict.
- An unresponsive audience could also be a signal that you are out of control.

Water

Is there anything more relaxing than the gentle song of flowing water? When the sun hangs high over the ocean, water reflects millions of tiny "diamonds" dancing on its surface. It seeks the lowest place, swirling around and over anything blocking its path.

Water conforms to whatever surrounds it and levels itself. Turn a bottle of Perrier on its side, upside down, on the other side, right side up. The water is always level. It also changes forms. Water can be liquid, steam, or ice.

Water connects cities, states, and continents.

It may be slow, but it is consistent. We may not think it is accomplishing much, but remember water carved through rock to create the Grand Canyon.

On a hot summer day, nothing refreshes like a cool stream or pool. Speaking of pools, water is also a lot of fun! It is cleansing. We bathe, wash our clothes, our food, and our living spaces with water.

Water is life sustaining. Like air, we cannot survive without water. It renews and invigorates. Just ask my poor, ignored houseplants. I never remember to water them until I see they have wilted. But after dousing them they return to their upright position.

Water is beautiful. I delight in playing tag with the lapping tide rolling in from the ocean deeps, enjoy the serenity of a placid lake, and admire the beauty of lacy snowflakes, sparkling raindrops, and cascading falls.

Behavior Traits Associated with Water

People who have the behavior traits of water can be described as *peaceful*. They are relaxed and thoughtful. They enjoy the company of others, but they also relish solitude, giving them time to reflect and think.

Water people are humble. If you need someone to listen to you, go to a water person. They are not comfortable in the spotlight, but like working behind the scenes. Like water, they seek the lowest place. They also seek the easiest way. If a problem or person blocks them, they will quietly find a way around the obstacle. They are consistent and quietly stubborn.

Just as water conforms to its container, water people conform to their surroundings. They are flexible, easy to please and fit in anywhere. The word, *whatever*, describes their mindset. In other words, "Whatever you want is fine with me."

In stressful situations, they have clear perspective and can keep a cool, level head, making them able to smooth things over. They are patient, even when provoked, and can put out the uncontrolled fury of fire people. They are great at public relation and as mediators because they can reflect all sides of the circumstance.

Water people are refreshing. Weary people seek them out to be renewed and invigorated, just like my wilted houseplants pleading for a drink.

Water Speaker Strengths

These speakers have a calm, conversational delivery, which immediately "connects" them with the audience. They speak as if they were having coffee with you in your kitchen. Water speakers are a pleasure to listen to because they can come up with insights rarely heard from the others. They are deep and thoughtful. Because they are observant their information is fresh and relevant to the times. These speakers can carry the burden of controversial subjects without offending their audience. One would never feel intimidated or looked down upon by these speakers because of their humility.

It doesn't matter the setting for the presentation, since the water speaker fits in anywhere. They give as earnest a presentation for five people as they do for five hundred. Water speakers are not "prima donnas" in that they are not demanding, but are easy to please. They will work with event coordinators and adjust wherever needed. Should someone from the audience become confrontational, the water speaker keeps a cool head, patiently mollifies the person, and flows on.

One of the water speaker's most gratifying pleasures is to help others succeed and to connect them with people and opportunities which will further their craft. After their presentation, the audience is invigorated and ready to use the information they've received. And because of the speaker's dry wit, they also have a merry heart.

Water Speaker Weaknesses

If water speakers are too laid back they run the risk of boring the audience. Their face lacks expression. Their arms either hang by their sides or are flopped on the podium. Their monotone voices can lull the audience to sleep. Heaven help these speakers if they draw an "after lunch" slot!

Because water speakers like to think, meditate, and reflect, they tend to procrastinate and wait until the last minute to put their program together. The same goes for practicing. They would rather flow around the obstacles of preparation and practice while hoping everything comes together. Their "it will be all right" attitude is a recipe for disaster, or at the very least, a slumbering audience.

Since these speakers are so careful to reflect all views, they can appear to have no opinion at all—sort of wishy-washy. They take the path of least resistance and say nothing at all. If the audience is unresponsive, these speakers either freeze or turn into a vapor and disappear.

Strengths to Build Upon:
- Your calm, conversational delivery.
- Your deep and thoughtful insights.
- Explore ways of addressing controversial subjects without offending the audience.
- Your ability to make others feel at peace and valued.
- Your goals to help others to succeed

Weaknesses to avoid:
- Being too laid back. Speak up and out, move, lean into the audience and talk to them.
- Watch out for slipping into a monotone voice. Vary it.
- Don't procrastinate! Put your program together and *practice!*
- Don't waver in your point, stick with it.

When Strengths Become Weaknesses:
- A calm, laid back personality taken to the extreme could appear indifferent and cold.
- Conforming, being able to see all sides might make you seem indecisive, destroying the trust of your audience.

Remember:
- Stay connected with your audience. Don't appear apathetic and passive
- Use expression in your face, body language, and voice.
- If your audience is unresponsive, don't freeze or disappear. Power through. You never know the real reason. Some may be so interested in

what you are saying they are trying to get every point. Others may have stayed up with a sick loved one all night, or may be in the middle of some kind of personal conflict.

Earth

This has to be my favorite universal element. The earth gives us many things. It protects and supports us. Earth gives us a place to stand, build our homes, and plant our gardens. It provides places for animals to escape their predators. Treasures of diamonds, emeralds, and rubies lie deep underground, waiting to be discovered. Gold, silver, and platinum are hidden in its layers.

Earth supports life. It provides shelter and food to sustain all living things. Every year Neal and I plant two large gardens. The plants spread their roots in the nourishing soil and produce an abundant crop. We enjoy the vegetables, as do the deer, rabbits, raccoons, and crows. Even with all those hungry mouths, we still have enough to can and enjoy throughout the year.

Earth is beautiful and creative. The majestic Rockies tower to the sky, purple with white caps, the Blue Ridge and Ozark Mountains so lush and green. My friend, Connie, has beautiful gardens with dozens of flower varieties. All the red, violet, gold, yellow, deep purple, orange, bronze, blooms and foliage enrapture me. The fragrances are intoxicating.

I travel a lot, and am always delighted by the many textures, and hues, of our wonderful earth. The desert hills of New Mexico are ribbons of red, orange, and brown. Ireland is lush and green. England is a feast of colorful gardens. Honduras is an orchard of banana trees, pineapple groves, and coffee bushes.

Earth is orderly. It has seasons and cycles unique for each hemisphere.

So, what does this tell us about the earth? It:
- Supports and protects.
- Contains treasure.
- Sustains life.

- Is beautiful and creative.
- Is orderly.

Behavior Traits Associated with Earth

Those who have behavior traits of earth are stable and grounded people. They are also very complex. They have many treasures hidden inside them, but you will not hear them bragging. In fact, you will have to dig to find their many talents. Most of our artists, musicians and poets have the traits of earth. Like the earth, they create beauty.

Earth people are nurturing and compassionate, however, they do not make friends quickly and only a select few are allowed in their "inner circle." They do not enjoy big crowds, rather preferring conversation with one or two at the most.

The earth is orderly and so is the earth person. Because they are analytical, they enjoy lists, charts, graphs, anything that promotes clarity and orderliness. When Neal and I first married, I didn't understand this about him. Our daughter, Amanda, used to watch for him out the front window and when she'd see him, she would run to the door. Neal walked in, passed Amanda and me, straightened the living room curtain and then gave us our kisses. That disturbed me, until I realized he couldn't help it—he was wired that way.

They are also deadline militants. I appreciate this about Neal because I often need a good kick in the pants to meet mine.

Earth people are intellectual, factual, objective, logical thinkers, and want details. They do not exaggerate and have little patience with those who do. Before they speak, they gather information—lots of information—and need feedback from others. They are reluctant to start anything. Instead, they make a long mental list of all the reasons they shouldn't. They are the first to see all the things that could go wrong as well as the impracticality and expense of a project. However, if someone else "plants the seed" and gets it started, earth people will certainly finish it. They do not like anything "undone." It drives them crazy.

This is the reason Neal and I work so well together. I am like the air. I scatter the seeds of idea and plant them in Neal. He finishes my projects while I scatter more seeds. Pity my husband.

Earth people have an interesting sense of humor. Most cannot tell a joke, but when they recount funny stories from their childhood or family, everyone is in stitches. I think the reason they are poor joke tellers is that they "over think" it.

They want everything perfect and set high standards for everything and everyone, including themselves. If they do not achieve their own standards they become insecure. Earth people also have a tendency toward negativity and depression. If only they could recognize what treasures they are, even with their flaws.

Earth Speaker Strengths

Earth speakers are the most conscientious and detailed of the four types. Their preparation for each speaking engagement is impeccable. They do exhaustive research making sure their facts are accurate and their information is practical. They use charts, graphs, and visual aids to present information in logical order. They set deadlines for themselves, have all preparation finished early and then practice until they get it perfect. The result? Their smooth delivery is always easy to follow and the audience understands the points of their presentation.

Because of their creativity and appreciation for the arts and nature, they often use photographs, current media clips and music in their presentations. It is obvious to those listening to them that earth speakers really care about their audience and will go to any length to help them.

Their humility and sincerity give them a connection with those to whom they are speaking because the audience trusts them and their information. Another endearing element of earth speakers is when they share anecdotes about their childhoods or families. They understand the effectiveness of these stories in furthering their points.

Earth Speaker Weaknesses

There are not many weaknesses to warn about for Earth speakers. However, there are a few things they need to watch for. They like to research and gather a lot of information and feel it *all* needs to be presented. It doesn't. If they try to give all of their information, they will either overwhelm their audience or bore them to tears.

Because they are perfectionists they tend to be stiff and inflexible. If anything goes wrong—and something usually does—or if they forget a fact, they freeze. Insecurities quickly take over and they stumble all over themselves for the remainder of their talk. Their attention to detail and perfectionism could even paralyze them from starting their presentation.

Earth speakers are not condescending, but they do tend to be negative. And this tendency could flavor the outlook of their presentation. Even their solutions can be depressing. Although the audience expects honesty, they also want a reason to hope.

Their reserve and self-consciousness hampers effective body language, resulting in stiff and choppy movements. This also hinders their ability to tell a joke. It would be wise to practice joke telling on family members first.

While speaking to audience members after their speech they can appear aloof. One reason is they often feel awkward in crowds. Also, because of their humility, they are uncomfortable receiving praise.

Strengths to Build Upon:
- Your attention to accurate information and details.
- Your commitment to being prepared.
- Your creativity.
- Telling relevant anecdotes about your childhood or family.

Weaknesses to avoid:
- Too much information
- Perfectionism. No one is perfect, no situation allows for perfection. Do your best and be satisfied.
- Being negative and self-conscious. Concentrate on your audience.
- Be gracious afterwards while speaking to people. Lean into them instead of pulling away.

When Strengths Become Weaknesses:
- Your thorough research can become overwhelming.
- Your attention to detail can paralyze you from even starting.
- Your humility could make you seem aloof and ungracious.

Remember:
- Remember this: *You only have time for a snapshot, not a movie.* Your greatest challenge is to decide what is important and what isn't

because as far as you are concerned, it is all vital information.

- Preparation is good; perfectionism can be a ball and chain around your neck.
- Humility is your strength, but learn to accept compliments graciously.
- If your audience is unresponsive, don't dig a hole and bury yourself. Power through. You never know the real reason. Some may be so interested in what you are saying they are trying to get every point. Others may have stayed up with a sick loved one all night, or may be in the middle of some kind of personal conflict.

How to Use a Speaker Profile Sheet

In my introduction to this chapter I mentioned it is rare when someone has behavior traits of one universal element exclusively. We are usually a blend of all of them, and two are dominant. For example, I behave like water and air. I consider those my dominant traits. However, if anyone messes with my family I will display the traits of a raging fire! But that isn't my day-to-day behavior. In my unguarded true self, I am like water. I reflect, meditate, think deeply, and am slow in deciding. This of course drives Neal crazy. Since he is like earth, he wants to produce! He is also fire. He wants to move fast. I can't count the times I've had to make a snap decision (or at least it felt like a snap to me) only to regret it later. And since I regretted it, so did Neal. He is learning to let me think.

I am also like air. I thrive on change, love to travel, and am sometimes hard to follow in a conversation. I may jump to three different subjects while talking to Neal. Poor guy. That's probably the reason his hair is thinning on top. He's constantly scratching his head wondering what the dickens I'm talking about.

Remember my example in the air profile section about cleaning closets. That's me. If I find a magazine, or even worse a photo album, I will sit there for hours while it only seems like minutes.

Knowing myself has not only improved me as a speaker, it has improved my communication in daily life. It also helps to understand others, especially our significant others. For instance, Neal has earth and fire traits. I have wind and water traits. When we had our yearly argument, (Yep, we've been married so long that we've pared it down to once a year. Frankly, that's all we have energy for) our disagreement always grew more heated and intense.

One day I pictured how his universal element and mine interacted in this situation. Neal behaves like fire and I behave like wind. Let me ask you, what happens when wind blows on fire?

- It makes it grow hotter and blaze bigger
- It spreads—fast
- It gets out of control

I realized that I needed to draw from my water behavior when our "discussion" grows a little heated. What does water do to fire?

- Cools it down
- Puts out the wildfire.

The profile sheet on the next page will help you identify your dominant traits, your strengths and potential weakness and develop a plan to improve your effectiveness as a speaker.

Hopefully, this knowledge will improve your communication in all spheres of your life.

Speaker Profile Sheet

List your behavior traits that are found in:

Air:

Fire:

Water:

Earth:

List the two universal elements that best describe your habits

1.

2.

List the strengths that best describe your habits for each one

1.

2.

List the weaknesses that best describe your habits for each one

1.

2.

List how the strength of one can help you overcome the weakness of the other:

1.

2.

List the strengths you want to build upon

List your plan for overcoming weaknesses

And Furthermore . . .

"The ability to express an idea is well nigh as important as the idea itself."~ Bernard M. Baruch

Although this book is small, it has a lot of information to digest. In this chapter I am going to make a bullet list of additional suggestions and to recap important points.

Before Your Presentation

- When you are invited to speak, ask for a contact name, their phone number (both landline and cell), the address and the room where the meeting will be held. I label a folder, "speaking engagements" and put all my information in it. This keeps everything in one place and is handy for when I need to refer to the engagement.
- Additional questions you might ask are:
  - How much time is allotted for you to speak. Knowing this will help you plan your talk. For instance, if you are given 30 minutes, you might speak 20-25 minutes and leave 5-10 minutes for questions. A 45-minute time allotment gives you 30-35 minutes with time left for questions.

- o Will you be using a microphone, and if so will it be hand-held or hands-free? This will help you know what to wear.
- o If you are speaking at an event with multiple presenters, ask what time you are speaking. Morning slots are no problem. However, if you are speaking after lunch or are the last one to present, it's harder to keep the audience's attention. Knowing when you speak will help you plan, and in the case of an after lunch slot, you will know that you need to add a few tricks to keep their interest. I'll give some suggestions in the next section.
- o What is the normal size of the group? This is nice to know if you are planning on making handouts.
- o The demographics of the group. Knowing this will alert you to the need for adjusting your talk to fit the audience.

- If you are speaking locally and are unsure of the event location, drive there a few days ahead of time to know the exact location.
- Try to arrive early to get a feel for the room and become acquainted with the sound-system. It is also good to mingle with people as they come in. Learn a few names so you can use them later. I'll explain in the next section.
- If you are going to have a book table, you must be there early. Be sure to put your One-Sheets and business cards on the table as well as your books.
- Ask a friend to be in charge of the table so you will be free to speak with members of the audience after you've finished.

- Be sure to bring enough change to give people who buy your merchandise.
- Inventory the books and other materials you plan to bring so you will know what you sold.
- If it is impossible to be early, BE ON TIME! I've been on both sides of the spectrum. It is miserable when the speaker is late because the success of the program depends on him or her. And the success of that program insures success of future programs. You have agreed to speak, so be responsible and arrive in a timely manner. If extenuating circumstances, like traffic backed up due to an accident, keep you from being on time, be sure to call your contact so they can rearrange the program in order to give you more time to arrive.
- Choose what you are wearing the day before, including accessories. Try everything on in front of a mirror and move as if you are speaking. Does anything bind your movements? Does your hem rise too high? Does your shirt come un-tucked and bunch over your belt? Are your shoes comfortable and do they add stability? Ladies, can you see through your skirt or dress? Does your neckline work its way down? If you bend over does it reveal too much? Is there a gap between the buttons across your chest? Does your bra color contrast against your skin and show through your dress or blouse? Does your jewelry rattle?
- A month or so before you speak check the event's website and make sure they haven't mistakenly changed your topic. I've had that happen twice and had to scramble to change my presentation. Once, I was slotted to give an extra presentation I hadn't planned on. Thank goodness I checked early!

- Provide your introduction to the person who is introducing you. Bring two copies in case one of them is lost or destroyed.
- If you are going to use some type of media, have a backup in case it fails. I attended a workshop where a presenter couldn't get her PowerPoint to work and we sat in the dark for twenty minutes while she fiddled with it. Miserable!
- Don't drink anything carbonated before you speak or eat foods that give you gas.
- PRACTICE! Read it over and over out loud until you are familiar with your material. Then practice from your outline. I put my note cards on the bar in my kitchen as if it were my podium and speak to the furniture in the living room. That way I can practice walking around. Finally, stand in front of a mirror and practice your body language while giving your talk. You may feel silly doing all this, but when you are in front of a crowd you will be so happy you did!
- When you arrive, ask for a bottle or glass of water to take to the podium if they haven't placed one there already. You might get a tickle in your throat.
- Before you step in front of everyone make sure buttons are buttoned and zippers are zipped.

During Your Presentation

- Relax! Remember, your audience is pulling for you. They want you to succeed. If you are nervous, they will be nervous for you. If you act like you just want to get this over with, they will tune you out. That is bad, because word of mouth gets around fast and others may be reluctant to ask you to speak for them.

- Do not tell the audience you are nervous.
- Never refuse to use a microphone. You may think you don't need it, but you do. Those in the back will have a hard time hearing you.
- Remember, it isn't about you! It is all about the audience. You are giving them something, you are providing a service, and that is why they are there. They don't care how tall or short you are, how thin or heavy you may be, or if your voice sounds like Kermit the frog. They want to hear what you came to say. Don't disappoint them.
- You are a writer! A storyteller. Connect with your audience by telling stories, anecdotes from your life, and using humor.
- Gauge your audience by reading their body language. If they are fidgeting or looking around the room, you may need to pick things up a bit and be more animated. If they are frowning and looking confused, you may need to slow down and try to be a little less technical. Don't worry about the occasional snoozer. There is one in every audience. One of my dear friends got her best beauty rest during meetings, no matter how dynamic the speaker.
- Some things to do if you get an after lunch, or late afternoon slot:
  - Ask questions and have something to give the first person with the correct answer. Something small such as a pen or a bookmark is suitable.
  - In the previous section I suggested you mingle with people as they walk in the room and learn their names. While speaking, use those names. If I'm speaking to a writer's group I might say something like, "We all want to be published some day, right Mark? I also

try to work in an observation I've made about an audience member. Let's say I'm speaking about using vivid description, I may say, "Barbara's shirt is blue, but it is better to say royal blue." Believe me, when the speaker is "calling names" everyone perks up.

- o If you can have them repeat a word or phrase after you, they will have to take in more oxygen helping them to stay awake.
- o Appropriate jokes or funny stories sprinkled throughout your talk will rejuvenate them when they laugh.

• Stay within your time limit. If you see that you are running over the allotted time you gave yourself, eliminate the question and answer period and give your email address for questions. Or you can answer them individually after the meeting.

• If you make a mistake, don't sweat it. Even our most eloquent government servants blunder sometimes. Vice-President, Joe Biden, was interviewed by CBS while he was still a senator. He made this statement on national television, "Franklin D. Roosevelt was president when the stock market crashed in 1929." *Problem is the president at that time was Herbert Hoover.* Biden also went on to say President Roosevelt went on television and explained what had happened. *Another problem, television as we know it didn't exist.* So, if you misspeak and catch it right away, correct yourself, laugh it off, and continue. Remember, a graceful recovery will keep the audience with you. Don't bother correcting small mistakes like when you say "yer". It will just draw the audience's attention away from your topic.

- If you forget part of your presentation keep in mind that the audience doesn't have your notes.
- Do not offer the freedom for audience members who have questions to raise their hands and ask at any time during your talk. Someone will, believe me and usually it is a person who will monopolize as much time as possible because she or he likes the attention. This only serves to eat up your time and makes you lose focus. Tell the group you will try and save time at the end for Q&A. If someone raises their hand, acknowledge them and reiterate that you will take questions at the end of your presentation.
- During Q & A *always repeat the question* so everyone can hear. Don't leave anyone out of the loop. You want them all to be included.
- If a person asks two questions, answer them as two separate questions. Repeat one, answer it, then repeat the other and answer.
- If you do not know the answer say so. If you'd like, offer to find out the answer, get the person's email address and get back with them.
- Use simple and relevant visual aids when appropriate. This not only will hold interest, it will aid in clarifying your talk and will make it memorable. Many years ago, I listened to Dr. Gary Smalley talk about treasuring our families. He wanted us to not only recognize their value, but to make it evident that we treasured them. The whole time he spoke he held a violin. It wasn't in the best of shape, and those with an untrained eye wouldn't place any value on it. Then he told us it was a Stradivarius. A soft gasp sounded across the room. We all recognized the worth of the violin

even in its shoddy state. At that moment, he encouraged all of us to gasp in awe whenever we see our mates and our children. I'll never forget that presentation.

- Handouts are great PR tools. Audiences love them. You can provide your outline so your audience can follow along. It is also a good idea to list all the URLs to avoid valuable time spelling them out. You might want to give additional information on your subject. These sheets also provide a place for them to take notes. Be sure your name and contact information is at the top of each one.

- A great way to end your presentation is to have a drawing for a free book. Provide forms with spaces for names and email addresses, plus a box to check if they want to be on your email address. Have them passed to the front and use them for the drawing.

After Your Presentation

- Remain up front and make yourself available for anyone who wants to speak with you for a moment.

- Make mental notes of compliments and use them on your one-sheets.

- As soon as you have some private time, review your presentation. Write down what worked and what didn't. Make a note of changes you would like to make and what you want to add.

- CONGRATULATE YOURSELF! You did it! Your platform is being constructed and you are on your way up!

Connect!

"Words mean more than what is set down on paper. It takes the human voice to infuse them with shades of deeper meaning" ~ Maya Angelou

How well I remember my first writers' conference. It was in the Ozarks during the fall. I came prepared. I stuffed my briefcase full with paper, sticky notes, pens, automatic pencils, highlighters, business cards, paper clips, and even a tiny stapler. The thing had to weigh forty pounds! But hey, I was a writer.

The speaker, an agent from New York, stepped up to the podium and surveyed the audience. His cavalier expression sent the clear message he was doing us hillbillies a favor.

For the next hour he dashed away every dream in the room by declaring to us that it is next to impossible to be published. He even gave statistics. Self-publishing? "Forget it," he said, "because self-published writers are not considered legitimate authors." In the end, he suggested we write letters. After all, that was writing, wasn't it?

After he stepped off the podium, I wanted to connect with him—by whopping him over the head with that forty-pound briefcase.

Even if he was right—and he wasn't—why didn't he give us options? Other than writing letters, that is. He should have told us about small presses. Why didn't he tell us about the many successful writers who self-published in the beginning of their writing career. He could have told us about POD (Print on Demand) publishers. Why didn't he give us some steps to improve our writing so we might catch the eye of an editor?

Over the years I've attended many writer's conferences. Each time I go, I carefully choose from the topics in the program that interests me. I'm anxious to hear the advice and tips the speaker will share. Imagine my disappointment when the speaker steps up to the podium and says, "I really don't know what you need, so I will just take questions." In other words this speaker was conveying this message to the audience, "I didn't think it worth my time to prepare something to give you so I'll just wing it by answering questions."

When that happens, inevitably some "bucket-mouth" in the audience monopolizes the meeting by making statements thinly disguised as questions, but what they really want to do is "teach the speaker." Other members ask about things that have nothing to do with the advertised topic. So for an hour I'm stuck listening to bucket-mouth and to information that has nothing to do with my writing.

This happens too many times. Now, when a speaker announces his or her program is going to be a Q & A session, I leave.

Don't be like these speakers! Please remember, the people came to hear you, not the person sitting in the crowd with them.

If you are a successful writer or when you become successful, remember the times you sat in the audience wanting to know how to be an author. Give them the gift of your experience. Give them the gift of encouragement. Take the time and prepare for them. Even if there are only three in the audience, give them the same as you would 300.

As you build others up, you are building your platform. Your reputation will grow and before you know it, you'll be in demand.

By connecting with your audience, you will connect with editors, agents, and publishing houses.

Stand up and speak out!

CONNECT!

Recommended Sites

AWOC.COM Publishing: www.awoc.com

Terry Burns: www.terryburns.net

Hartline Literary Services: www.hartlineliterary.com

Velda Brotherton: www.veldabrotherton.com

Dusty Richards: www.dustyrichards.com

Jane Kirkpatrick: www.jkbooks.com

Nita Beshear: www.nitabeshear.com

Northwest Arkansas Writers: www.nwawriters.org

Florence Littauer:
www.classervices.com/FlorenceLittauer.html

CLASServices: www.classervices.com

Toastmasters: www.toastmasters.org

Special Note:

If the chapter on speaking styles intrigued you, and you are interested in a personality profile using the elements, I recommend Laurie Beth Jones' book: *The Four Elements of Success*. Even though the focus in this book is on corporations and team building, as Laurie Beth points out, families *are* teams. There is also an online assessment available at a reasonable cost and I encourage you to take it before reading the book. You will receive a comprehensive evaluation of your temperament type with a graph charting out the percentage of each element you exhibit and thorough explanation.

Of all the temperament tests I've taken and studied, this one by far is my favorite. It is easy to identify, remember, and understand.

Laurie Beth has many other products and services that enhance communication and understanding. For more information please visit her website at: www.lauriebethjones.com.

Inspire! Writing from the Soul

*A drop of ink may make a
million think.* ~ Mark Twain

Did you enjoy this book? You may also enjoy *Inspire! Writing from the Soul* by Linda C. Apple.

Inspirational writing is one of the fastest growing markets today. Uplifting life experience stories are in demand for publications like:

- *Chicken Soup for the Soul*
- *Cup of Comfort*
- *God Allows U-Turns*
- Magazines
- Devotional Guides
- and many more

Find out what it takes for your story to catch the eyes of publishers and connect with the hearts and minds of your readers. Learn how to inject emotion, the five senses, and purpose into your life experience stories, devotionals, articles, and fiction.

Motivational speaker and inspirational writer, Linda Apple, offers practical instruction for those who want to write with passion and purpose. Inspire! Writing from the Soul is an excellent resource for small writing groups and individuals as well.

www.AWOCBooks.com?b=69

CPSIA information can be obtained at www.ICGtesting.com
Printed in the USA
LVOW091011180712

290553LV00001B/38/P